CW01654500

SNAP SCIENCE

GET YOUR TEETH INTO IT!

Teacher's Guide
Year 5

William Collins' dream of knowledge for all began with the publication of his first book in 1819.

A self-educated mill worker, he not only enriched millions of lives, but also founded a flourishing publishing house. Today, staying true to this spirit, Collins books are packed with inspiration, innovation and practical expertise. They place you at the centre of a world of possibility and give you exactly what you need to explore it.

Published by Collins
An imprint of HarperCollins*Publishers*

The News Building, 1 London Bridge Street, London, SE1 9GF, UK

Macken House, 39/40 Mayor Street Upper, Dublin 1, D01 C9W8, Ireland

Browse the complete Collins catalogue at
collins.co.uk

10 9 8 7 6 5 4 3 2 1

ISBN 978-0-00-868521-8

British Library Cataloguing-in-Publication Data

A catalogue record for this publication is available from the British Library.

Authors: David Allen, Nicola Beverley, Naomi Hiscock, Liz Lawrence, Jules Pottle and Claire Seeley

Series Editor: Jane Turner

Publisher: Laura White

Packager: Oriel Square

Cover designer: Amparo at Kneath Associates

Production controller: Alhady Ali

Printed and Bound in the UK by Ashford Colour Press Ltd

MIX
Paper | Supporting responsible forestry
FSC™ C007454

This book contains FSC™ certified paper and other controlled sources to ensure responsible forest management.

For more information visit: www.harpercollins.co.uk/green

collins.co.uk/sustainability

Acknowledgements

The publishers gratefully acknowledge the permission granted to reproduce the copyright material in this book. Every effort has been made to trace copyright holders and to obtain their permission for the use of copyright material. The publishers will gladly receive any information enabling them to rectify any error or omission at the first opportunity.

Contents

Introduction to *Snap Science*

What is *Snap Science*?

Snap Science is a comprehensive and rich resource that provides everything primary schools need to plan, teach and assess the National Curriculum for primary science. It has been written by a team of leading experts who have spent years teaching science in primary schools, working with trainees, delivering professional learning for teachers and subject leaders, carrying out research, developing resources and advising policy makers and curriculum designers. Each of them is passionate about primary science: they know how important it is for primary children to develop secure knowledge of the big ideas in science, to learn how scientists work to build that knowledge and how that knowledge can be used to meet the global changes we face. They know how exciting it is to be in a primary classroom when science is being well taught: where children are connecting their learning, finding things out through practical experimentation, using scientific vocabulary to explain what they know and seeing the relevance of their learning to their lives.

They also know how challenging it is to lead and teach primary science well, and what a responsibility that is. It is not easy to plan a curriculum which is made up of complex ideas in Biology, Chemistry and Physics as well as the disciplinary knowledge of working scientifically, which includes practical work and outdoor learning, and which needs to build positive attitudes as well as secure learning.

So that is why they created *Snap* – to give teachers the resources that will develop the confidence, skills and knowledge to teach science well.

What is the *Snap* framework?

- A complete long-term plan for science which fully covers the National Curriculum and is constructed to ensure clear progression of knowledge and skills year by year.
- Medium-term plans for each year group, organised as six modules where the learning has been broken into straightforward, cognitively appropriate steps to be taught and assessed lesson by lesson.
- Between four and eight lesson plans per module.
- Resources to support teachers to plan, teach and assess science effectively.
- The realisation of the *Snap* vision for science: for all children to make sustained progress, securely learning new knowledge and skills and connecting then to prior learning, exploring the world through practical experimentation, building positive attitudes to science and seeing the relevance of their learning to their lives and how it can help build a better future for all.

How has the long-term plan been designed?

The *Snap* long-term plan provides subject leaders with a coherent curriculum for science, from Year 1 to Year 6. The National Curriculum has been broken into modules which are organised logically to ensure that all substantive and disciplinary knowledge is taught and learnt well, at an appropriate time of the year and in an order which is underpinned by a clear progression. Scientific ideas, skills and vocabulary have all been sequenced to make sure that children's learning builds on prior understanding.

What are *Snap* lessons like?

Each lesson is framed by a question – often a science enquiry question. In the lesson, children are taught new knowledge to enable them to answer that question. In many lessons they also collect data using an enquiry type to help then answer the question. In each lesson, formative assessment strategies are used to elicit children's prior knowledge, so that learning is progressive. Every lesson ends with a 'reflect and review' activity where children summarise their learning.

Each lesson is designed to teach a part of or a complete National Curriculum substantive knowledge statement, and for children to make progress towards meeting relevant working scientifically statements. Assessment indicators are provided to enable teachers and children to make accurate judgements about the progress that has been made.

Enquiry types are used appropriately, and working scientifically skills are explicitly taught and used, with clear links made to how scientists, including named historical and contemporary figures, work.

Clear guidance for teachers is provided to use a range of evidence-informed teaching strategies, including practical work, use of Tier 3 vocabulary, teacher demonstration, direct teaching, enquiry-based learning, modelling, drama, outdoor learning, and dialogic teaching.

Practical, logistical information is included about timing, teaching spaces and equipment.

Teaching is enriched with videos, interactives, slide shows, resource sheets and images. Learning activities are clearly outlined and resources are provided for collecting data, recording observation and summarising learning.

What other support for subject leaders and teachers is there?

The *Snap* Pupil Workbooks and printed Teacher's Guides can be used alongside the *Snap* digital subscription available on Collins Hub. As well as editable versions of the lesson plans in this book, there are module summaries, PowerPoints, videos, animations, assessments and resource sheets, and comprehensive teacher support and CPD.

What is in each module summary?

Each module contains everything a teacher needs to teach a topic.

The **National Curriculum statements** taught in each module have been broken into a detailed progression of learning. The science that children will learn in each lesson is clearly stated as well as how teachers will assess that learning, using evidence from what children do in the lesson. There are additional assessment activities called Snapshots that teachers can use if they are unable to make an assessment judgement based on what children write, say, draw or model in the classroom.

The **subject knowledge** teachers need to make sure that their own understanding is strong and their explanations are accurate is included. Scientific misconceptions children (and teachers) may hold are listed with the correct version given. The **scientific vocabulary** (Tier 3) that children will learn and use in the lessons is listed with age-appropriate definitions, as well as any non-science specific words (Tier 2) that may be needed to fully engage with the lesson.

Vital information is included to guide teachers to teach in ways that will build all children's **science capital**, valuing children's knowledge, ideas and experiences, and developing their capacity to use their science learning in their lives now and in the future. Meaningful **links to other subject areas** are made, including carefully selected books for children to read to enhance their science learning. Full **resource lists**, created to be sustainable, affordable and meet health and safety guidance are included.

What support is there for science leaders?

Leading science using *Snap* is a useful summary of how *Snap Science* enables confident and enjoyable leadership of science. Read this for information about how *Snap* supports subject leaders to meet Ofsted 2023 recommendations for curriculum design, progression and best practice in teaching, learning and assessment in their school.

For further information about the *Snap* approach there are briefings to explain the *Snap* understanding of best practice science teaching and learning and what has informed it. These summarise current evidence-based guidance about **Working scientifically**, **Assessment**, **Sustainability**, **Equality, diversity and inclusion** and **Integrating literacy**. These are also available as short, summary presentations which you can use in staff meetings.

The ***Snap*** **long-term plan** shows how the National Curriculum is organised for Years 1–6. The ***Snap*** **Progression charts** for **Conceptual knowledge** and **Working scientifically** provide a lot more detail. **Planning using *Snap*** and **Teaching and assessing using *Snap*** are important documents to share with teachers as they provide full guidance for using the *Snap* framework. These are also available as ten-minute summary presentations which you can use in staff meetings.

There are also examples of **Module summaries** and **Lesson plans** with quick-reference annotations explaining how to use the guidance in the different sections.

The ***Snap* assessment trackers**, one per year, enable teachers to track children's progress easily throughout the year, and are presented as Excel spreadsheets so that you can integrate information with your school's own systems if necessary. Instructions for using it are in **Teaching and assessing using Snap**.

The **Glossaries** of the science-specific vocabulary, one for each year, are useful reference documents for teachers, giving simple definitions for each word appropriate to the year, with progression baked in.

The **Resources lists** will make sure that everyone is well prepared with everything they need to teach great lessons.

Lesson overview

Lesson	Workbook page
Module 1: Forces and mechanisms	
Lesson 1: What is the friction between different surfaces? Friction is a force that makes it harder to move an object across a surface or slows down an object moving over a surface. The force of friction can be measured using a Newton meter. The unit of measurement of a force is Newtons (abbreviated to N).	*2*
Lesson 2: Why do some objects fall faster than others? Gravity is a force that pulls all objects towards the centre of the Earth. Air resistance is a force that slows down an object moving through air. The amount of air resistance depends on the surface area of the object. It is air resistance, not the object's weight, that affects how quickly an object falls.	*5*
Lesson 3: How does the size of the canopy affect the time it takes a parachute to fall? This lesson consolidates the understanding that air resistance increases as the surface area of the object moving through the air gets larger. The precision of a measurement will depend on the equipment and method used. The accuracy of readings shows how close they are to the true answer and is improved by taking repeat readings and keeping variables the same.	*7*
Lesson 4: How does the shape of an object affect its movement in water? Water resistance is a force that slows down an object moving through water. The amount of water resistance depends on the shape of the object.	*10*
Lesson 5: How does the number of pulleys affect the force needed to lift a load? A pulley is a mechanism used for lifting heavy objects (the load) by applying a pulling force at one end of rope attached to the load which passes over a wheel. The more pulleys in the mechanism, the less pulling force is required to lift the load.	*12*
Lesson 6: How does the length of the lever affect the force needed to lift a load? A lever is a long, rigid arm that rests on a pivot. A force is applied to one part of the lever to lift the load at another point on the lever. The longer the lever, the less force is required to lift the load.	*14*
Lesson 7: How do gears work? A gear is a mechanism which consists of wheels with teeth that slot together. Gears change the direction of movement and the force required to make something move. Adjacent gears turn in opposite directions. Smaller gears turn faster than larger gears. A smaller force is needed to turn a smaller gear than a larger gear.	*16*
Module 2: Properties and uses of materials	
Lesson 1: How can we compare and group materials? Materials have properties that make them fit for certain purposes. These may include being: absorbent, brittle, durable, ductile, elastic, electrical conductor, electrical insulator, flexible, hard, malleable, transparent, translucent, opaque, permeable/impermeable, rigid, thermal conductor, thermal insulator, magnetic.	*18*
Lesson 2: Which materials did the builders use when constructing our school and why? Materials are used in many different ways and for particular purposes based on their properties. Materials can be fit-for-purpose. How materials may vary in form (e.g. plastics of different types) and why they are used for particular purposes. Weathering, wear and tear can occur over time and this will have an impact upon a material's fitness-for-purpose.	*21*
Lesson 3: Which liquid is the thickest? Liquids have properties which include having: [a fixed weight, a fixed volume,] an ability to flow, a level of viscosity and they take on the	*24*

shape of a container. Viscosity is the property of a liquid that describes how fast or slowly it will flow. The viscosity of a liquid describes how thick or thin it is. A liquid with high viscosity (thick) will flow slowly and a liquid with low viscosity (thin) will flow quickly.	
Lesson 4: Who invents things? Inventors discover new uses for materials and create new materials. Inventors design objects using their knowledge of the properties of materials.	***27***
Lesson 5: Can the same container keep cold things cold and hot things hot? A thermal insulator is a material that provides high resistance to heat flow. Examples include rubber, wool, wood, polystyrene/foam, plastics. A thermal conductor is a material that provides low resistance to heat flow. Examples include metals, such as aluminium, copper, steel, and iron. A thermal insulator keeps hot things hot and cold things cold.	***30***
Lesson 6: Which materials are absorbent, permeable or waterproof? Materials can be absorbent and can soak up and take in liquid. Some materials are permeable and let water pass through. Some materials are waterproof and do not let water pass through. The use of some materials can have an impact on the environment.	***34***
Module 3: Earth and space	
Lesson 1: What's in space? The main bodies that are found in our solar system are the Sun, Moon, Earth and planets. They are all spherical.	***36***
Lesson 2: How do the planets move? The Earth orbits the Sun. The time it takes to complete one orbit is called a year. The other planets of our solar system also orbit the Sun at different distances and take different times to complete one orbit.	***38***
Lesson 3: How does the position of the Sun in the sky change? The Sun appears to move east to west in an arc across the sky from sunrise to sunset. Changes in shadows during the day can be explained by the changes in the position of the Sun.	***40***
Lesson 4: What causes day and night? The Earth rotates on its axis and this causes day and night, the apparent movement of the Sun across the sky and the changes in shadows observed in Lesson 3.	***42***
Lesson 5: How does the Moon move? The Moon orbits the Earth every 28 days and rotates on its axis.	***43***
Lesson 6: What patterns can we find in data about the planets? Check and consolidation of conceptual learning from Lessons 1–5. Children may notice, but do not need to explain, the phases of the Moon. They do not need to learn about the tilt of the Earth causing seasonal changes; this will be taught in Key Stage 3.	***46***
Module 4: Plant and animal life cycles	
Lesson 1: How do flowering plants produce seeds? All living things have a life cycle which includes growth and reproduction, eventually ending in death and decay. Flowers contain male sex organs called stamens and female sex organs called carpels. Pollen must be moved to a part of the carpel called the stigma for reproduction to take place. This process is called pollination. Seeds are the product of sexual reproduction.	***50***
Lesson 2: Do all plants have the same number of reproductive parts? Most flowering plants have flowers with both male and female parts – such as tulips, daisies and roses. Different flowers have different numbers of petals, stamens or carpels. r.	***53***
Lesson 3: How can we grow more plants without using seeds? Asexual reproduction creates new plants that are identical to the parent. Bulbs, tubers, runners and plantlets are new plants which grow from parts of existing plants. Gardeners may make more plants by taking cuttings, growing new plants from small parts of a parent plant.	***56***
Lesson 4: How do birds change over their lifetime? Most animals reproduce sexually. This involves two parents a male and a female. The sperm from the male fertilises the female egg inside her body. Female birds lay eggs with hard shells. These may or may not be fertilised.	***58***

Module 1: Forces and mechanisms

Lesson 1: What is the friction between different surfaces?

What children will learn and do

- Children learn that friction is a force that makes it more difficult to move an object across a surface, or slows down a moving object.
- They learn how to use a force meter to measure friction.
- They make predictions about the friction between different surfaces.
- They answer the lesson question: **'What is the friction between different surfaces?'**

You will need

- magnets to demonstrate attraction and repulsion (optional)
- magnetic and non-magnetic materials, including magnetic and non-magnetic metals (optional)
- rectangular pieces of rough sandpaper, approximately 10 × 5 cm (one per group)
- rectangular pieces of tin foil, approximately 10 × 5 cm (one per group)
- large matchboxes, each filled with modelling clay; aim for each filled box to weigh the same amount (one per group)
- a toy vehicle
- 2.5 N force meters (one per group)
- force meters with a different scale: 5 N, 10 N or 20 N (one per group)
- sets of materials to provide different surfaces, for example, rough sandpaper, tin foil, rectangular sections cut from rubber gloves or thin foam rubber, cotton cloth (one set per group)

If using the Snap Science Year 5 Pupil Workbook you may not require all the resource sheets below.

Snap Science Year 5 Pupil Workbook

- pages 2–4

Snap Science Year 5 Digital subscription

- Resource sheet 1: Forces: true or false?
- Resource sheet 2: Recording table (optional)

Make sure you have opened/printed any Snap resources you intend to use in this lesson.

National Curriculum

Conceptual knowledge:

- identify the effects of [air resistance, water resistance and] friction, that act between moving surfaces

Working scientifically:

- using test results to make predictions to set up further comparative and fair tests
- taking measurements, using a range of scientific equipment, with increasing [accuracy and] precision, taking repeat readings when appropriate

Scientific enquiry type:

- comparative testing

Key vocabulary	
Tier 2 vocabulary:	Tier 3 vocabulary: comparative test, dependent variable, enquiry, independent variable, precise, predict force, force meter, friction, Newton (N)

Health and safety Please refer to CLEAPSS for Health and Safety guidance and ensure that any identified hazards are managed appropriately.

Getting started

Organise children into groups of three. Give each group a set of cards cut out from Resource sheet 1: Forces: true or false? Ask them to decide whether the statements on the cards are true or false. This should remind them of what they learnt about forces in Year 3 (Module 3, Forces: friction and magnets). After the card sort, ask children which statements they are sure about and why. Clarify any that they were not sure about. If needed, use magnets and magnetic/non-magnetic materials to demonstrate that the statements involving magnetism are true/false.

Give each group a rectangle of rough sandpaper and a rectangle of tin foil (each roughly 10 × 5 cm). Encourage them to talk about how the materials feel. Ask children which surface would be better for a playground slide and why.

Show the children a large matchbox filled with modelling clay (to give it more weight). Ask them which surface it will be easier to drag the box across: the sandpaper or the tin foil. Ask them to explain why.

Explain to children that there is a 'rubbing' force acting between the bottom of the box that is being dragged and the surface that the box is resting on. This force is called friction. Demonstrate friction another way by giving a toy vehicle a push to get it rolling along a table. Explain the following: Friction between the wheels and the table will slow the vehicle down and bring it to a stop. Friction is a force that makes it more difficult to move an object across a surface, or slows down an object moving over a surface. The rougher the surface, the greater the friction.

Show children some different force meters, for example, 2.5 N, 5 N, 10 N and 20 N. Give each group of children two different force meters to compare. Ask them what is the same about the two force meters and what is different.

Tell children to look at the size of the spring and of the scales. Ask them to pull the hook and feel how much force is required to stretch the spring. They should observe that it is harder to stretch the force meters with spring with thicker coils and that these ones have scales that give higher numbers. Explain the following: Force meters measure a force. The unit of measurement is Newtons, named after Sir Isaac Newton. This is abbreviated to N. You need to choose the correct force meter depending on the size of the force that is being measured. If it is a large force, you will need a force meter with a larger scale so that the needle does not go beyond the scale. If you are measuring a small force, you will need one with a smaller scale so that the needle does not register zero Newtons. Choosing the correct force meter is important for taking precise measurements. The precision of measurements will depend on the equipment used to take them. For example, if measuring a period of time, the measurements will be more precise if you use a stopwatch than if you use a sand timer.

Explain that children should use only the Newton scale (there may also be a gram-force scale) and check it is set at zero before taking each reading.

Demonstrate how to use the hook on the force meter to attach it to the weighted matchbox and drag it across the table. Demonstrate this using force meters with different scales and ask children to identify the most suitable one to use to take precise readings.

Ask one or two children to look closely at the needle as the box starts to move, is moved at a constant speed and is left to rest. They should observe that initially the force is larger when the box starts to move and then remains constant as the box is pulled at a steady speed and then returns to zero when the box stops moving. Repeat this a couple of times with different children observing and ask them to read the value carefully when the box is moving at a steady speed. This should be the same each time. Explain that you have repeated the test a number of times, but, as the values were the same or very similar, it is not really necessary to repeat the test.

Pupil Workbook: Complete Activity 1: True or false? on page 2 and Activity 2: Reading force meters on page 2.

The task

Tell children that today's question is: **'What is the friction between different surfaces?'** Explain that they will answer this question by measuring the force required to drag the box over different surfaces. Explain that one child will need to hold the surface in place on the table, another uses the force meter to pull the box at a constant speed and other group members read the value on the force meter scale.

Ask children what type of enquiry they think they will be using to gather evidence to answer the question (comparative testing). Ask them to identify the independent variable – the thing they are changing (the material the box is moving over) – and the dependent variable – the thing they are measuring (the force of the friction).

They will be working like scientists as they will be collecting and interpreting data to answer scientific questions.

Organise children into groups of three or four. Give each group a large matchbox filled with modelling clay and a selection of materials to be used as different surfaces (for example, rough sandpaper, tin foil, rectangular sections cut from rubber gloves or thin foam rubber, cotton cloth).

Ask children to draw a table in their books to record their data. Before they start testing, ask them to write the materials into the table according to how much friction they predict each will provide. They should write one they predict will give the lowest friction first, and then write the others in order, finishing with the one they predict will give the highest friction. Remind children that they are working like scientists, as scientists often use the knowledge they already have to predict results of their tests.

When the children have measured the force for each surface and recorded it in their table, ask them to answer the question: **'What is the friction between different surfaces?'** Provide the sentence structure: 'As the texture of the surface … the force of friction produced … This is because …'

Pupil Workbook: Complete Activity 3: What is the friction between different surfaces? on page 3 and Activity 4: Conclusion on page 4.

Adaptations and support

Children could be provided with a template for their table, on Resource sheet 2: Recording table.

Take it further

Children could find other types of surfaces in the classroom to test. Encourage them to predict a value before testing.

Reflect and review

Remind children of today's lesson question: **'What is the friction between different surfaces?'**

Ask one group to read out the materials of the surfaces according to how much friction they produced, starting with the smallest amount of friction. Ask other groups if their results match this order. They probably do, which shows that the results are trustworthy as more than one group got the same results. The exact values may vary from group to group, due to different amounts of modelling clay being used or the size of the box.

Ask children to write a definition of the word 'friction' in their books.

Ask children to discuss examples in their everyday life where friction plays a role. In each example, is it desirable to have high or low friction?

Pupil Workbook: Complete Activity 5: What is friction? on page 4.

Answers

Getting started:

Resource sheet 1: Forces: true or false

1. Forces make things move. **TRUE** – *They can, but they also do other things.*
2. You need a force to stop things moving. **TRUE**
3. A rubber mat would be the best thing to sit on to go fast down a slide. **FALSE**
4. The rougher the surface, the slower the movement. **TRUE** – *This is often true, but not always. Some objects may not move on very smooth surfaces as they will slip.*
5. Things stop moving because they are tired. **FALSE**
6. Forces can change the direction of movement of an object. **TRUE**
7. Forces can change the shape of an object. **TRUE** – *This was covered in Year 2 (Module 5, Changing materials).*
8. Forces can change the speed of an object. **TRUE**
9. Forces only make objects slow down. **FALSE**
10. Magnetism is a contact force. **FALSE**
11. A hard push makes a toy car travel further than a small push. **TRUE**
12. A push is an example of a non-contact force. **FALSE**
13. Forces cannot be measured. **FALSE** – *This is covered in this lesson.*
14. Friction makes things hot. **TRUE** – *This can be demonstrated by rubbing hands together.*
15. All metals are magnetic. **FALSE** – *Only some metals are magnetic (for example, iron and other materials such as stainless steel that contain iron).*
16. Big magnets have a stronger magnetic force than small magnets. **FALSE**
17. If you bring two magnets together, the north pole of one magnet attracts the south pole of the other. **TRUE**

The sandpaper is a rougher surface than the tin foil. In Year 3, children learnt that objects slide more easily on smooth surfaces, so therefore the tin foil will be the better surface for sliding on. It will be more difficult to pull the box over the rougher surface – the sandpaper. The rougher the texture of the surface, the bigger the force of friction produced. This is because the bobbles on the surface make it harder to move the box across it.

Homework suggestions

Children could take a photograph or draw a picture of an example of friction having an impact on something at home or that they notice near to where they live.

Assessment and evidence of learning

Children can:

- use a force meter to measure the force of friction
- use their knowledge to predict the ranking of the surfaces
- record their results in a table
- use their results to write a conclusion to the enquiry
- explain the term 'friction' and give examples of surfaces that produce high and low friction.

Lesson 2: Why do some objects fall faster than others?

What children will learn and do

- Children learn that gravity is a force that pulls all objects towards the centre of the Earth.
- They learn that air resistance is a force that slows down an object that is moving through air.
- They learn that it is air resistance, not an object's mass, that affects how quickly it falls.
- They identify independent and dependent variables and use these to write scientific enquiry questions.
- They answer the lesson question: **'Why do some objects fall faster than others?'**

You will need

- a table tennis ball
- a golf ball
- two sheets of A4 paper
- a parachute made by attaching four strings to the corner of a piece of plastic (e.g. cut from a plastic bag) and joining the other ends of the strings together using a ball of modelling clay or adhesive tack

Snap Science Year 5 Pupil Workbook

- pages 5–6

Snap Science Year 5 Digital subscription

- Slideshow 1: Why do objects fall at different speeds?
- Snapshot 1: What is gravity?

Make sure you have opened/printed any Snap resources you intend to use in this lesson.

National Curriculum

Conceptual knowledge:

- explain that unsupported objects fall towards the Earth because of the force of gravity acting between the Earth and the falling object
- identify the effects of air resistance, [water resistance and friction,] that act between moving surfaces

Working scientifically:

- planning different types of scientific enquiries to answer questions, including recognising and controlling variables where necessary
- identifying scientific evidence that has been used to support or refute ideas or arguments

Scientific enquiry type:

- comparative and fair testing

Key vocabulary	
Tier 2 vocabulary:	**Tier 3 vocabulary:** comparative test, dependent variable, enquiry, fair test, independent variable, refute, support air resistance, contact force, force, gravity, impact, non-contact force

Health and safety Please refer to CLEAPSS for Health and Safety guidance and ensure that any identified hazards are managed appropriately.

Getting started

Hold an object up in the air, for example, a pen. Ask children what will happen if you let go of it. They should say that it will fall to the ground. Drop the object and ask children to discuss why it falls to the ground. Remind them that if something moves, a force must be involved. If necessary, explain that the force in this instance is gravity. Explain that gravity is a force that pulls all objects towards the centre of the Earth and that it is a non-contact force.

Display Slideshow 1: Why do objects fall at different speeds? Show slide 1. Explain to children that almost 2,500 years ago in Greece, Aristotle thought that heavier objects fall faster than lighter objects. Galileo, 400 years ago in Italy, thought that all objects fall at the same speed, no matter how heavy. Ask children to discuss the statements with their partner. Who do they agree with? Can they explain why or give examples to support or refute the statements?

Show children a table tennis ball and a golf ball. Ask: What is the same about them and what is different? Ask them to vote for what will happen if the two balls are dropped at the same time from the same height. Will they land together, will the golf ball land first, or will the table tennis ball land first?

Drop both balls from the same height at the same time. They should land at the same time. You may need to repeat this several times, or ask children to repeat it, so that they accept that you are not 'cheating'. It is a very common misconception that heavier objects fall faster. Refer back to slide 1 and ask children to explain whether this provides evidence to support or refute either of the statements. Agree that the evidence refutes Aristotle's statement that heavier objects fall faster.

Now show the children two pieces of A4 paper and scrunch one into a small ball. Explain that they are the same mass but different shapes. Ask the children to vote for whether the two pieces of paper will land at the same time, the flat piece first, or the ball first.

Drop both pieces of paper from the same height at the same time. The ball should land first. Again, you may need to repeat this a few times. Refer back to slide 1 and ask children to explain whether this provides evidence to support or refute either of the statements. Agree that the evidence supports Galileo's statement that it is not the mass that makes the difference. It is something else – the shape of the object.

Explain the following: As well as gravity pulling downwards, another force acts upwards. When an object is falling, this force acts in the opposite direction to gravity. This force is air resistance. Air resistance is a force acting on all objects that are moving through air, whether the object is falling, moving along or rising. Air resistance always acts in the opposite direction to the direction the object is moving. It is a contact force. Show the three diagrams on slide 2 to clarify this.

Tell children that today's question is: **'Why do some objects fall faster than others?'** Ask them to explain in their books the evidence that they have seen that supports or refutes Aristotle's and Galileo's statements in order to answer this question.

Show children a parachute, made by attaching four strings to the corner of a piece of plastic and joining the other ends of the strings together using a ball of modelling clay or adhesive tack. Ask children what it is and what its purpose is (to slow down a falling object to reduce the impact when it hits the ground). Explain that the impact is the force produced when two objects collide. Demonstrate dropping the parachute and name its parts – canopy, strings and 'body' (the modelling clay).

Pupil Workbook: Complete Activity 1: Falling objects on page 5.

The task

Tell children that they are going to generate some questions that can be used to explore how a parachute works and to gather further evidence to support Galileo's statement in the next lesson.

Ask children to think back to the previous lesson to recall what independent variables and dependent variables are (independent variables are the ones that you change, dependent variables are the ones that you measure). Explain that they will be identifying independent and dependent variables and then using these to generate questions.

In their books, ask children to write the heading 'Independent variables' and to write down things that they could change about the parachute, how it is dropped or anything else that they think might affect how it falls.

Either gather ideas from each group or ask children to share their ideas with others on the table, allowing them to add ideas they get from other people to their list perhaps, using a different colour.

Then ask children to add a second heading: 'Dependent variables'. Ask them to write down what they could measure or observe to judge how the parachute falls. Again, allow time for children to hear ideas from others and add further ideas to their list if they wish. Remind them that the dependent variable should give information about how the parachute fell differently when something was changed. For example, the size of the canopy is not a dependent variable; it is an independent variable and will not change as the parachute falls. Ask children to check their list and cross off any that they now think are not dependent variables.

Show slide 3, which shows a range of gapped questions. Ask children to identify which colour boxes indicate the independent and dependent variables. (Yellow = independent; blue = dependent.)

Ask children to use their identified variables to record a range of different scientific questions in their books. Explain that they will make use of these questions in the next lesson.

Pupil Workbook: Complete Activity 2: Identifying variables on page 5.

Adaptations and support

Children can be given one question stem repeated so that they can simply add in the independent and dependent variables.

Take it further

Children could be encouraged to consider which questions would provide further evidence to support Galileo's statement and to explain how they would carry out the enquiry.

Reflect and review

Ask some of the children to share one of their questions and ask other children to identify the independent and dependent variable.

Remind children of today's question: **'Why do some objects fall faster than others?'** Ask them which questions will provide further evidence for this. Ask them which type of enquiry they would use to answer these questions (comparative testing or fair testing).

Children have worked like scientists as they have identified evidence to support or refute statements and have identified variables to help them to generate scientific questions.

Answers

The task:

Possible independent variables (not an exhaustive list):

- area of canopy
- material of canopy
- shape of canopy
- length of strings

- material of strings
- mass of body
- shape of body
- height from which it is dropped

Possible dependent variables (not an exhaustive list):

- time taken to reach the floor
- distance moved from vertical
- path of the parachute (observation)
- impact on landing
- sound on landing

Teachers should be aware that it is a fair test when the variables are continuous data that can be measured, for example, independent variables such as the height the canopy is dropped from and length of strings, and dependent variables such as time taken to fall and distance moved from vertical. A line graph could be drawn to present the data. It is a comparative test where the variables are not continuous data, for example, independent variables such as the material of the canopy or of the strings, and dependent variables such as the path of the parachute and what happens to it (impact) on landing. Results would be presented in a table. (It is not necessary for children to learn this distinction.)

Homework suggestions

Children could take a copy of slide 1 home to discuss with members of their family who they agree with and then show them evidence to refute Aristotle's idea and support Galileo's.

Assessment and evidence of learning

Children can:

- explain the terms 'gravity' and 'air resistance'
- explain that the speed at which an object falls depends on air resistance not mass
- identify independent and dependent variables for an enquiry
- generate scientific questions.

If you are unsure if a child can explain that unsupported objects fall towards the Earth because of the force of gravity acting between the Earth and the falling object, you can use Snapshot 1: What is gravity? to check understanding and develop the learning.

Lesson 3: How does the size of the canopy affect the time it takes a parachute to fall?

What children will learn and do

- Children consolidate knowledge that air resistance increases as the surface area of the object moving through the air gets larger.
- They identify which line graph matches their prediction.
- They use a stopwatch to time how long a parachute takes to reach the floor.
- They learn to use repeat readings to increase the accuracy of measurements.
- They evaluate their data and use it to write a conclusion.
- They answer the lesson question: **'How does the size of the canopy affect the time it takes a parachute to fall?'**

You will need

- four parachutes, each made by attaching four strings to the corner of a piece of plastic (e.g. cut from a plastic bag) and joining the other ends of the strings together using a ball of modelling clay or adhesive tack; for each parachute, the piece of plastic should be identical in size, but folded in half each time to create a different-sized canopy but without changing the weight; ensure the length of the strings and the size and shape of the attached 'body' are the same
- stopwatches (one per pair of children)

If using the Snap Science Year 5 Pupil Workbook you may not require the resource sheet below.

Snap Science Year 5 Pupil Workbook

- pages 7–9

Snap Science Year 5 Digital subscription

- Slideshow 1: Line graphs
- Resource sheet 1: Recording table (optional)

Make sure you have opened/printed any Snap resources you intend to use in this lesson.

National Curriculum

Conceptual knowledge:

- identify the effects of air resistance, [water resistance and friction,] that act between moving surfaces

Working scientifically:

- taking measurements, using a range of scientific equipment, with increasing accuracy and precision, taking repeat readings when appropriate
- reporting and presenting findings from enquiries, including conclusions, causal relationships and explanations of and degree of trust in results, in oral and written forms such as displays and other presentations

Scientific enquiry type:

- comparative and fair testing

Key vocabulary	
Tier 2 vocabulary:	**Tier 3 vocabulary:** accuracy, comparative test, conclude/conclusion, enquiry, evaluate, fair test, independent variable, line graph, precise, predict, variable

	air resistance, contact force, force, friction, gravity, magnetism, non-contact force

Health and safety Please refer to CLEAPSS for Health and Safety guidance and ensure that any identified hazards are managed appropriately.

Getting started

Ask children to discuss in pairs what contact forces and non-contact forces are and to give examples. Ask pairs to share their ideas and ensure that friction and air resistance are named as contact forces and magnetism and gravity are named as non-contact forces and that they can define each of these forces.

Remind children of the question from the previous lesson: 'Why do some objects fall faster than others?' Ask them to explain the answer to this to their partner, possibly using a diagram if this helps. Ensure that children remember that it is the amount of air resistance that affects how fast an object falls, not its weight.

Explain that today they are going to explore how to change the amount of air resistance. Ask children to review the list of independent variables that they identified in the previous lesson and decide which one they think will have the greatest effect on how quickly the object falls (that is, the variable that will have the greatest effect on the air resistance). Hopefully they will suggest the size of the canopy, but if necessary remind them of the demonstration in the previous lesson of dropping the flat and scrunched-up pieces of paper.

Show children the parachutes that you have made. The first should have the piece of plastic unfolded; the second should have the plastic folded in half; the third should have the plastic folded in quarters; and the fourth should have the plastic folded in eighths. Ask children to look at their list of independent variables and identify what variables they will need to keep the same (all the others). Explain that all the parachutes are the same weight as you have folded identical-sized pieces of plastic in order to make the parachutes of different sizes.

Tell children that today's question is: **'How does the size of the canopy affect the time it takes a parachute to fall?'** Ask them to use what they know about air resistance to predict the answer.

Display Slideshow 1: Line graphs. Tell children that line graphs are a way of presenting data, where the variable that is being changed (the independent variable) is a continuous number. The area of the canopy may be 10 cm^2 or 20 cm^2 or anything in between, for example, 14.9 cm^2. Ask them to discuss the shape of each graph and what this means. For example, the first graph shows that as the size of the canopy increases, it does not make any difference to the time that it takes for the parachute to reach the floor. Graphs 2 and 4 show that the time increases as the canopy gets larger, but graph 4 indicates that it takes no time for the body to fall if there is no canopy. Graph 3 shows that as the canopy gets larger the time it takes to fall decreases. Graph 5 shows the time decreasing and then increasing with size. Graph 6 shows the time increasing and then decreasing with size.

Ask children to decide which graph shape matches their prediction and to record this in their book explaining why they have chosen this one.

Pupil Workbook: Complete Activity 1: How does the size of the canopy affect the time it takes a parachute to fall? on page 7.

The task

Remind children of today's question: **'How does the size of the canopy affect the time it takes a parachute to fall?'** Ask them what type of enquiry they think they will be using to gather evidence to answer the question (comparative testing or fair testing).

Give each pair of children a stopwatch and ensure that they know how to start, stop and reset it. Have a few practice tries where you drop the parachute and children time it to establish a suitable procedure, for example, you saying 'three, two, one' and dropping it on 'go'.

Remind children that when they were testing friction by dragging a box across different surfaces, they found that it was not necessary to take repeat readings as each repeat reading was very similar. Ask children whether they should do repeat readings for this activity. Explain that they should take more readings if the measurements are more varied.

Ask children to draw a table to record the data. If necessary, show them how to add further columns to record up to five repeat readings.

Start by dropping the smallest parachute from above your head, asking the children to record how long it takes to reach the floor. Ask whether this should be repeated. Repeat either three or five times depending on how variable the measurements are. Be guided by the children on this.

Repeat for the other three parachutes in turn.

Pupil Workbook: Complete Activity 2: Results on page 8.

Adaptations and support

Children can be given Resource sheet 1: Recording table to collect the evidence. This includes a column for children to record the area of each parachute – complete this column for the children.

Take it further

Children could be encouraged to calculate the area of the canopy of each parachute.

Reflect and review

When the testing is complete, ask children to look at their results for each parachute and draw a circle around the measurement that would be the middle reading if they were put in order. You may need to model this if they have not learnt about finding the median average in maths. If they have, remind them that this is what they are doing. Alternatively, if they have already learnt how to work out the mean average you could ask them to calculate this for each parachute. Ask children to add a further column to their table to record this average for each parachute.

Remind children of today's lesson question: **'How does the size of the canopy affect the time it takes a parachute to fall?'** Ask children to look at the average time for each parachute and identify whether the data will produce the same shape graph that they predicted earlier on in the lesson.

If there is not a big difference in the size of the canopies, or the height from which they were dropped is not great, it is quite likely that the results for all the parachutes will be very similar and therefore the data seems to match graph 1, more than graph 2. Discuss why this might be. The bigger the range of size of canopies and the greater the height they are dropped from, the more likely it is that the evidence will support the prediction that the time increases as the area increases due to the increase in air resistance.

Use the following sentence starters to talk through a conclusion and evaluation for the enquiry. Remind children that precision depends on the equipment and method used. Explain that accuracy is associated with how close to the true answer measurements are and is improved by taking repeat readings and keeping variables the same.

- I expected the time for the parachute to land to ... as the size of the parachute ... because ...
- The data supports/refutes this because ...
- We increased the precision of our measurements by ...
- We increased the accuracy of our measurements by ...

- I could improve my data by ...

Remind children that they have been working like scientists as they have gathered data and evaluated whether the data is sufficient to answer the question.

Ask children to discuss examples in their everyday life where air resistance plays a role. For each example, ask: Is it desirable to have a high or low air resistance?

Pupil Workbook: Complete Activity 3: Looking at your results on page 8 and Activity 4: Conclusion and evaluation on page 9.

Answers

Reflect and review:

Examples of how children might complete the sentences:

- I expected the time for the parachute to land to increase as the size of the parachute got larger because the surface area of the canopy moving through the air is bigger which means the air resistance is larger and slows the parachute down more.
- The data supports this because [give values to show the increase]./The data refutes this because [give values to show that the time did not change significantly].
- We increased the precision of our measurements by saying out loud, 'Three, two, one, go'.
- We increased the accuracy of our measurements by taking repeat readings and keeping variables such as [list of variables such as the weight of the parachute] the same.
- I could improve my data by dropping the parachute from a greater height and by increasing the range of the size of the parachute.

Homework suggestions

Children could repeat the activity using parachutes with a larger area range and dropping them from a greater height to see if they can improve the data gathered.

Assessment and evidence of learning

Children can:

- make a prediction based on their understanding of air resistance
- explain how they increased the precision of their measurements
- explain how they increased the accuracy of their measurements
- use the data gathered to write a conclusion
- evaluate how to improve the data gathered.

Lesson 4: How does the shape of an object affect its movement in water?

What children will learn and do

- Children learn what water resistance is and use this knowledge to make predictions.
- They decide how many repeat readings to take to increase the accuracy of the measurements.
- They find either the mean or median average.
- They evaluate their data and use it to write a conclusion.
- They answer the lesson question: **'How does the shape of an object affect its movement in water?'**

You will need

- digital scales to weigh the pieces of modelling clay out in advance of the lesson
- six balls of modelling clay, each weighing the same
- pieces of modelling clay each weighing the same (three per group)
- stopwatches (one per group)
- 1,000 ml measuring cylinders (one per group)
- 1,000 ml measuring jugs (one per group)
- paper towels
- a clear, viscous liquid, e.g. bubble bath, shower gel or shampoo

If using the Snap Science Year 5 Pupil Workbook you may not require the resource sheet below.

Snap Science Year 5 Pupil Workbook

- pages 10–11

Snap Science Year 5 Digital subscription

- Video 1: Moving in water
- Resource sheet 1: Recording table (optional)
- Snapshot 1: Air resistance, water resistance and friction: compare and contrast

Make sure you have opened/printed any Snap resources you intend to use in this lesson.

National Curriculum

Conceptual knowledge:

- identify the effects of [air resistance,] water resistance [and friction,] that act between moving surfaces

Working scientifically:

- using test results to make predictions to set up further comparative and fair tests
- reporting and presenting findings from enquiries, including conclusions, causal relationships and explanations of and degree of trust in results, in oral and written forms such as displays and other presentations

Scientific enquiry type:

- comparative testing

Key vocabulary	
Tier 2 vocabulary:	**Tier 3 vocabulary:** accuracy, accurate, conclude/conclusion, enquiry, evaluate, precise/precision, predict, refute, support air resistance, force, oppose, water resistance

Health and safety Please refer to CLEAPSS for Health and Safety guidance and ensure that any identified hazards are managed appropriately.

Getting started

Remind children that in the previous lesson they explored how air resistance affects how easily an object moves through air. Ask them what they found out and establish that the larger the surface area of the object, the greater the air resistance.

Ask children to talk about when they have tried to move in water. Ask: What different ways can you move in water? Which methods make it easier to move?

Explain the following: When an object is moving through water, a force called water resistance slows the object down or makes it harder to move. Water resistance is a force that opposes any movement through or on the surface of water. It can be defined as the force of the water pushing back against an object moving through it.

Ask children if they think it is easier to move through air or through water. Ask them to share their ideas. Play Video 1: Moving in water, which shows people on the beach and in the sea. Ask children to look for examples in the video to support the statement, 'It is easier to move through air than through water'.

Show children a measuring cylinder filled with 1,000 ml of water and two balls of modelling clay that are identical in weight. Ask children to suggest a way to use these resources to gather further evidence to support the statement, 'It is easier to move through air than through water.'

Demonstrate dropping the two balls from the same height, but one into the cylinder through the water and one outside of the cylinder through the air. You may wish to repeat this a few times, so have pairs of balls ready to save emptying out the cylinder in between.

Ask children to draw two diagrams in their books, one showing the forces acting on the ball moving through the water, and one showing the forces acting on the ball moving through air.

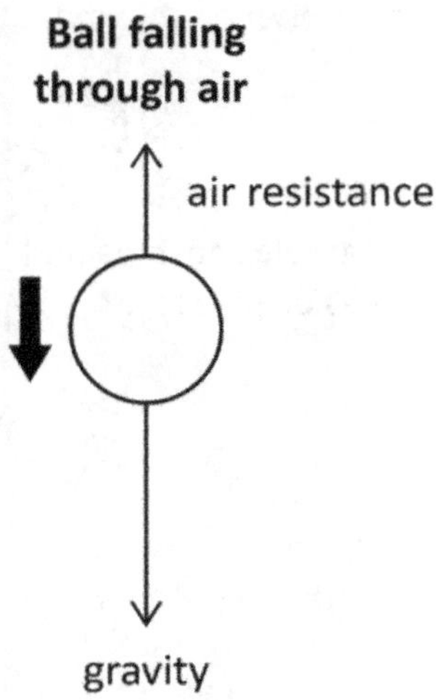

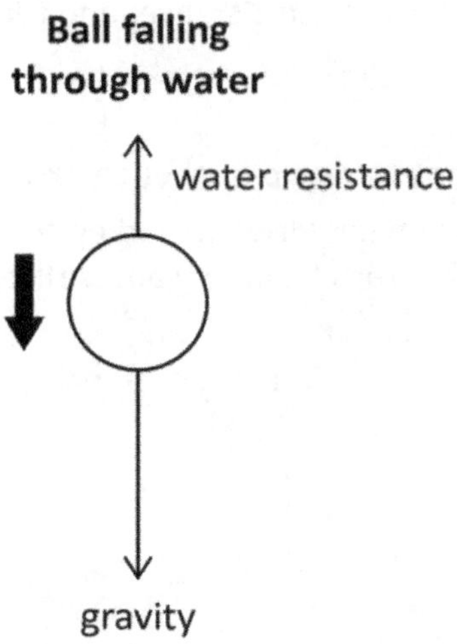

The task

Tell children that today's question is: **'How does the shape of an object affect its movement in water?'** Ask them to record this in their books. Ask them what type of enquiry they think they will be using to gather evidence to answer the question (comparative testing).

Explain that they are going to gather evidence to answer this by dropping pieces of modelling clay into a cylinder of water. Remind children what they learnt in the last lesson about taking precise and accurate measurements. They will need to think about the method they use to get precise timings. They will also need to think about how to ensure they keep all variables other than the shape of the object the same, and whether they need to take repeat readings and, if so, how many.

Give each group three balls of modelling clay, each identical in weight. Explain that you want them to change the shape of two of the balls to make one a shape that they think will move faster through the water than the ball and the other into a shape that will move more slowly through the water than the ball. Ask them to draw the three shapes that they will be testing in their books and explain why they think one shape will go faster and one slower than the ball. Remind them that they should use their understanding of water resistance and apply what they learnt about air resistance to make this prediction.

Give each group a 1,000 ml cylinder, a 1,000 ml jug filled with water (a little more than 1,000 ml) and a stopwatch.

Explain that they should test all three shapes first, then empty the water from the cylinder back into the jug to retrieve the shapes. The cylinder can then be refilled for repeat readings, as necessary.

Ask children to create a table to record their results before they start, referring back to the table they used in the previous lesson if necessary.

Give children a defined amount of time to gather their evidence, to ensure efficient working.

At the end of the allocated time, ask children to work out the median or mean average time for each shape and to consider whether the data supports or refutes their original predictions.

Pupil Workbook: Complete Activity 1: How does the shape of an object affect its movement in water? on page 10 and Activity 2: Results on page 11.

Adaptations and support

Children can be given Resource sheet 1: Recording table to collect the evidence, and to write their conclusion and evaluation.

Take it further

Children could be encouraged to suggest ways to improve the data gathered.

Reflect and review

Remind children of today's question: **'How does the shape of an object affect its movement in water?'** Ask them to look at the average time for each shape to fall and to identify whether the data they gathered supports or refutes their earlier predictions. Allow them to share their findings.

As in the previous lesson, the data may or may not show a great enough difference between the results to be sufficient to answer the question or support/refute children's predictions. Show and discuss the model evaluation and conclusion from the previous lesson:

- I expected the time for the parachute to land to increase as the size of the parachute got larger because the surface area of the canopy moving through the air is bigger which means the air resistance is larger and slows the parachute down more.
- The data supports this because [give values to show the increase]./The data refutes this because [give values to show that the time did not change significantly].
- We increased the precision of our measurements by saying out loud, 'Three, two, one, go'.
- We increased the accuracy of our measurements by taking repeat readings and keeping variables such as [list of variables such as the weight of the parachute] the same.
- I could improve my data by dropping the parachute from a greater height and by increasing the range of the size of the parachute.

Ask children to write an evaluation and conclusion for today's enquiry using the same sentence structures.

Remind children that in the previous lesson they discussed how, by dropping the parachute from a greater height and by increasing the range of the size of the parachute, they may have improved their results. Ask any children who carried this out for homework to tell the class whether it did improve the results. Ask children to think about how they could improve the results today. The problem is that the shape gets to the bottom of the cylinder too quickly. What could they do?

Demonstrate pouring a more viscous (thicker) liquid than water (for example, shampoo or bubble bath) into a measuring cylinder. Ideally, this should be clear or light in colour. Ask children how this is different to water. Demonstrate dropping two identical balls of modelling clay at the same time into a cylinder of the viscous liquid and a cylinder of water to compare. The ball in the viscous liquid moves more slowly as there is more 'water' resistance as the liquid is thicker. Explain that repeating the test using an even thicker liquid would give clearer results.

Remind children that they have been working like scientists as they have gathered data and evaluated whether the data is sufficient to answer the question.

Pupil Workbook: Complete Activity 3: Conclusion and evaluation on page 11.

Answers

Getting started:

What different ways can you move in water? Which methods make it easier to move? If the water is shallow, it is possible to walk through the water. As the water gets deeper, it gets harder to walk. It is easier to jump forward rather than walk. It is easier to swim or push off the edge and glide than it is to walk.

Homework suggestions

Children could repeat today's activity using bubble bath or another thick liquid to see if they can improve the data gathered. They can use a 1.5 litre plastic bottle with the top cut off as a cylinder. An adult should cut the top off and cover the edge with masking tape to prevent injury on the sharp edge.

Assessment and evidence of learning

Children can:

- make a prediction based on their understanding of water resistance
- explain how they increased the precision of their measurements
- explain how they increased the accuracy of their measurements
- use the data gathered to write a conclusion.

If you are unsure if a child can identify the effects of air resistance, water resistance and friction, that act between moving surfaces, you can use Snapshot 1: Air resistance, water resistance and friction: compare and contrast to check understanding and develop the learning.

Lesson 5: How does the number of pulleys affect the force needed to lift a load?

What children will learn and do

- Children learn that a pulley is a mechanism that is used to lift heavy objects by applying a pulling force at one end of rope attached to the load which passes over a wheel.
- They learn that the more pulleys in the mechanism, the less pulling force is required to lift the load.
- They decide how many repeat readings to take to increase the accuracy of the measurements.
- They use their data to write a conclusion and make further predictions.
- They answer the lesson question: **'How does the number of pulleys affect the force needed to lift a load?'**

You will need

- a large matchbox, filled with modelling clay
- an identical matchbox filled with modelling clay, with 'wheels' added; create the wheels by sticking two drinking straws to the base, threading a thin wooden skewer through each one, and attaching four plastic bottle lids (e.g. milk carton lids) to the ends of the skewers using adhesive tack; the bottle lids will need to have small holes punched through the middles (alternatively, you could use parts of a construction kit)
- a one-litre milk carton filled with sand
- lengths of dowelling (one per group)
- empty cotton reels (or curtain rings) (two per group)
- coat hangers, bent as shown on slide 3 of Slideshow 1 (one per group)
- balls of string (one per group)
- one-kilogram weights with handles (one per group)
- force meters with a range of scales

If using the Snap Science Year 5 Pupil Workbook you may not require all the resource sheets below.

Snap Science Year 5 Pupil Workbook

- pages 12–13

Snap Science Year 5 Digital subscription

- Slideshow 1: Pulleys
- Resource sheet 1: Recording table (optional)
- Resource sheet 2: Pulley data: spreadsheet
- Video 1: Cranes in action

Make sure you have opened/printed any Snap resources you intend to use in this lesson.

Note that Resource sheet 2 is a spreadsheet, into which you can enter the results of the children's enquiries in order to generate a bar chart. If you have fewer than eight groups of children, you will need to edit the formulas in cells J2, J3, J4 and J5.

National Curriculum

Conceptual knowledge:

- recognise that some mechanisms, including levers, pulleys and gears, allow a smaller force to have a greater effect

Working scientifically:

- using test results to make predictions [to set up further comparative and fair tests]

- reporting and presenting findings from enquiries, including conclusions, causal relationships [and explanations of and degree of trust in results, in oral and written forms such as displays and other presentations]

Scientific enquiry type:

- comparative testing

Key vocabulary	
Tier 2 vocabulary:	**Tier 3 vocabulary:** accuracy, comparative test, enquiry, precise/precision, predict force, friction, load, mechanism, pulley

Health and safety Please refer to CLEAPSS for Health and Safety guidance and ensure that any identified hazards are managed appropriately.

Getting started

Ask children what they think a mechanism is. Explain that a mechanism is a device that makes it easier to move something. Ask them to think about moving a heavy load, such as a packed suitcase. Ask: What do many suitcases have added to them to make them easier to move? Explain that a wheel is a simple mechanism.

Ask children what force the wheels are reducing. (Friction.) Ask them to think back to Lesson 1 when they measured friction and compared the amount of friction produced by different surfaces. Demonstrate that wheels reduce friction by using a force meter to measure the force required to pull a large matchbox weighted with modelling clay, and then an identical weighted matchbox with wheels. You could also demonstrate moving the box over rollers (round pencils or dowelling placed under the box, as shown in the image below).

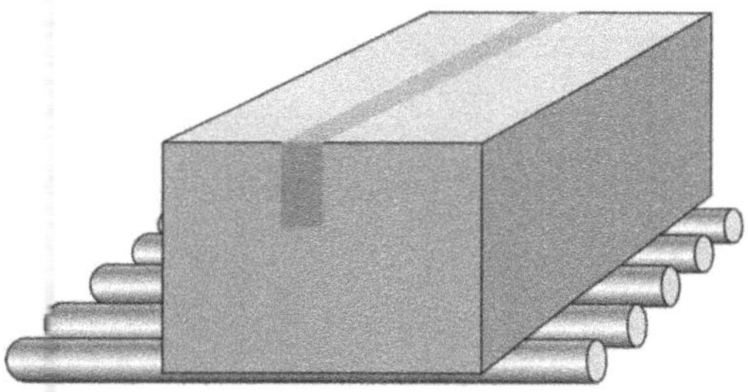

Explain to children that they are going to investigate another type of mechanism that helps with lifting (don't use the term 'pulley' yet). Demonstrate a simple pulley: lift a one-litre plastic milk carton filled with sand off the floor, using string tied to the handle. Measure the force with a force meter. Lift it again, pulling the string over a length of dowelling held by a child at each end. Measure the force. Finally, thread the dowelling through an empty cotton reel and repeat the lift with the string over the cotton reel. (Alternatively, a curtain ring could be used instead of the cotton reel: thread the dowelling through the curtain ring, then thread the string through the ring.) Measure the force. Ask children if the force changed. Both lifts are examples of simple pulleys, but the lift over the dowelling alone might give a higher force reading than the straight lift because of friction between string and dowel. The measurement with the cotton reel should be about the same as the straight lift. While the lifting force is the same, it is easier to pull down than to pull up.

Tell children that this is a mechanism called a pulley. Explain that a pulley is a mechanism used for lifting a heavy object (a load) by applying pulling force at one end of rope which passes over a wheel. Prompt children to think of anywhere they have seen pulleys used, and what they were used for.

Display Slideshow 1: Pulleys. Show slide 1. If the classroom has blinds, demonstrate how pulleys are used to lift and lower them. While still displaying slide 1, ask children to draw a diagram showing a pulley system and to label the pulley, the rope, the load and the pulling force.

Show slide 2 and explain that often more than one pulley is used. Ask children to identify the number of pulleys in each image.

Pupil Workbook: Complete Activity 1: How do pulleys work? on page 12.

The task

Tell children that today's question is: **'How does the number of pulleys affect the force needed to lift a load?'** Ask them to write this in their books. Ask them what type of enquiry they think they will be using to gather evidence to answer the question (comparative testing).

Show slide 3, which shows how to create the mechanisms with different numbers of pulleys. Explain that children will be measuring the force required to lift a weight using one, two, three and four pulleys.

Remind children that they need to think about how to gather evidence they can trust to answer the question. Ask them to think about the activities in the previous lessons and how they increased the precision and accuracy of the readings. Ask them to draw a table to record their results including repeat readings, if they decide these are necessary.

Give each group a coat hanger, bent as shown in the diagrams on slide 3, a one-kilogram weight, a ball of string, a piece of dowelling and two cotton reels (or two curtain rings). This will allow each group to set up each system following the diagrams on slide 3. Alternatively, set up the systems in advance for the groups to rotate around.

Each group will also need a range of force meters with different scales.

As children are taking their measurements, ask them to explain why they have chosen to take repeat readings or not. Also observe whether they are choosing the most appropriate force meter to take the measurements.

Pupil Workbook: Complete Activity 2: How does the number of pulleys affect the force needed to lift a load? on page 12.

Adaptations and support

Children can be given Resource sheet 1: Recording table to collect their data.

Take it further

Children could be encouraged to draw a graph to present their results. This should be a bar chart as it is showing discrete (non-continuous) data.

Pupil Workbook: Complete Activity 3: Plotting your results on page 13.

Reflect and review

Remind children of today's question: **'How does the number of pulleys affect the force needed to lift a load?'** Ask them to discuss the answer to the question based on the evidence they have gathered. Ask some groups to share what they found out.

Gather the data from each group (just the average force for each number of pulleys) into Resource sheet 2: How does the number of pulleys affect the force needed to lift a load? Look at the data gathered by each group. Ask: Does it show the same pattern? The data should show that as the number of pulleys increases the force required to lift the load decreases.

Look at the graph. Ask children to use the graph to predict values for five, six and seven pulleys.

Ask children to answer in their books today's question: **'How does the number of pulleys affect the force needed to lift a load?'** Then ask them to record their predictions for the pulling force needed to lift the same load using five, six and seven pulleys. (The sentence structure shown in the Answers section below could be written on the board to support children.)

Remind children that they have been working like scientists as they have gathered data to answer the question and used the data gathered to make further predictions.

End the lesson by playing Video 1: Cranes in action.

Pupil Workbook: Complete Activity 4: Conclusion on page 13.

Answers

Reflect and review:

The data shows that as the number of pulleys increases, the force required to lift the load decreases. I predict that using five, six and seven pulleys the forces required will be ..., ... and ...

Homework suggestions

Children could look for examples of pulleys in their homes or outside and take photographs to share with the rest of the class.

Assessment and evidence of learning

Children can:

- draw a labelled diagram of a simple pulley
- measure a force, choosing the force meter with the most appropriate scale
- explain why they decided to take a chosen number of repeat readings
- use the data gathered to answer the enquiry question
- use the data gathered to make further predictions.

Lesson 6: How does the length of the lever affect the force needed to lift a load?

What children will learn and do

- Children learn that a lever is a mechanism that is used to lift heavy objects.
- They learn that a lever is a long, rigid arm that rests on a pivot and that a force is applied to one part of the lever to lift the load at another point on the lever.
- They decide how many repeat readings to take to increase the accuracy of the measurements.
- They use their data to write a conclusion.
- They answer the lesson question: **'How does the length of the lever affect the force needed to lift a load?'**

You will need

- an empty metal tin with an inset lid, e.g. a golden syrup or treacle tin, or a paint tin
- metal spoon or flathead screwdriver
- weights (one per group)
- elastic bands (one per group)
- string (one piece per group)
- rigid plastic or wooden rulers (one per group)
- force meters with a range of scales

If using the Snap Science Year 5 Pupil Workbook you may not require all the resource sheets below.

Snap Science Year 5 Pupil Workbook

- pages 14–15

Snap Science Year 5 Digital subscription

- Slideshow 1: Levers
- Resource sheet 1: Recording table
- Resource sheet 2: Lever data: spreadsheet

Make sure you have opened/printed any Snap resources you intend to use in this lesson.

Note that Resource sheet 2 is a spreadsheet, into which you can enter the results of the children's enquiries in order to generate a bar chart. If you have fewer than eight groups of children, you will need to edit the formulas in cells J2, J3, J4 and J5.

National Curriculum

Conceptual knowledge:

- recognise that some mechanisms, including levers, pulleys and gears, allow a smaller force to have a greater effect

Working scientifically:

- recording data and results of increasing complexity using scientific diagrams and labels, [classification keys, tables, scatter graphs, bar] and line graphs
- reporting and presenting findings from enquiries, including conclusions, causal relationships [and explanations of and degree of trust in results, in oral and written forms such as displays and other presentations]

Scientific enquiry type:

- fair testing

Key vocabulary	
Tier 2 vocabulary:	**Tier 3 vocabulary:** accuracy, control variable, dependent variable, fair test, independent variable, precise/precision, predict force, fulcrum, lever, load, mechanism, pivot, pulley

Health and safety Please refer to CLEAPSS for Health and Safety guidance and ensure that any identified hazards are managed appropriately.

Getting started

Remind children that in the last lesson they learnt about mechanisms, which are devices that make it easier to move something. Ask children to discuss with their partner what they learnt about pulleys. They should recall that a pulley is a simple mechanism used to lift heavy loads by applying a pulling force at one end of a rope which passes over a wheel. As the number of pulleys is increased, the force needed to lift the load is reduced.

Show children a metal tin with an inset lid, such as a treacle tin. Invite a child to try to open it. Ask children whether they have ever seen an adult open a tin like this. Ask: How did they do it? What did they use to help them open it? Show children how to use a metal spoon or a screwdriver to lift off the lid. Explain that you are using the spoon/screwdriver as a lever, which is another simple mechanism which makes it easier to move a load. The load in this case is the lid.

Display Slideshow 1: Levers. Show slide 1 and explain that the screwdriver is the lever and the hand pushing down on the handle is providing the force to lift the lid (the load) off the tin.

Show slide 2 and explain the following: The screwdriver rests on the edge of the tin. The handle is being pushed down but the other end of the screwdriver pushes up on the lid. The screwdriver pivots on the edge of the tin. This is called the fulcrum. The fulcrum of a lever is the point about which it turns.

Demonstrate how to set up a simple lever as shown on slide 3.

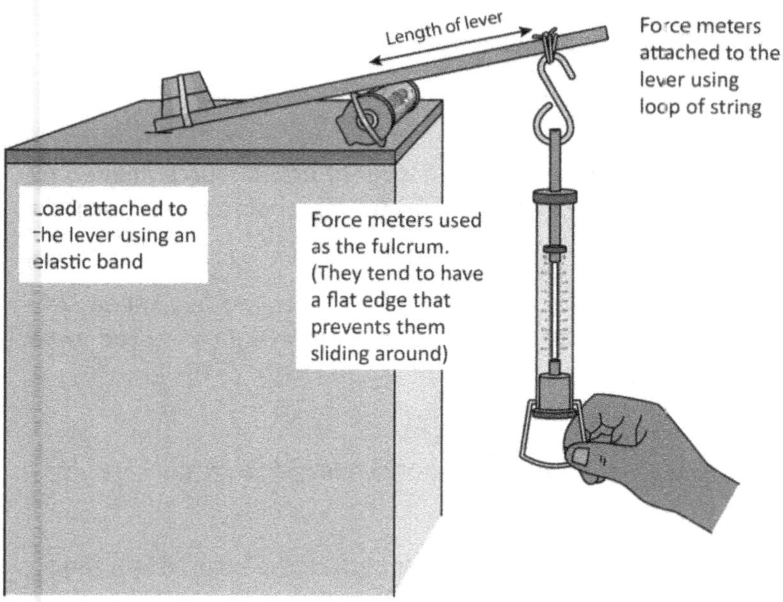

The task

Tell children that today's question is: **'How does the length of the lever affect the force needed to lift a load?'** Ask them to record this in their books. Explain that to do this they will carry out a fair test. They will keep the load and the fulcrum in the same place (the control variables) and change the position of the force meter pulling down on the lever (the independent variable). They will measure the forces required to lift the load (the dependent variable). Show slide 3 to clarify the distance that they will measure as the length of the lever. It is the distance from the fulcrum to the force meter, not the position of the force meter on the ruler.

Remind children that they need to think about how to gather evidence they can trust to answer the question. Ask them to think about the activities in the previous lessons and how they increased the precision and accuracy of the readings. Ask them to draw a table to record their results, including repeat readings if they decide these are necessary.

Give each group a range of force meters with different scales and a ruler with a weight attached to one end using an elastic band, and a piece of string tied on the other end which can be moved along the ruler which will be used to attach the force meter to the lever.

Ask them to set up the lever and carry out their tests, recording their evidence using Resource Sheet 1: Recording table.

Pupil Workbook: Complete Activity 1: How does the length of the lever affect the force needed to lift a load? on page 14.

Adaptations and support

To make it easier for the children to measure the length of the lever, attach the weights at 0 cm on the ruler and place the fulcrum at the 10 cm position on the ruler. Explain that they will need to subtract 10 cm from each measurement of the length of the lever.

Take it further

Children could be encouraged to draw a graph to present their results. This should be a line graph as it is showing continuous data.

Pupil Workbook: Complete Activity 2: Plotting your results on page 15.

Reflect and review

Remind the children of today's question: **'How does the length of the lever affect the force needed to lift a load?'** Ask them to discuss the answer, based on the evidence they have gathered. Ask some groups to share what they found out.

Gather the data from each group (just the average force for each lever length) into Resource sheet 2: How does the length of the lever affect the force needed to lift a load? Look at the data gathered by each group. Ask: Does it show the same pattern? The data should show that as the length of the lever increases, the force required to lift the load decreases.

Look at the graph. Ask children to use the graph to predict the lifting force needed to lift the same load using a longer lever of 25 cm or 30 cm.

Ask children to answer in their books today's question: **'How does the length of the lever affect the force needed to lift a load?'** They should also draw a labelled diagram of a lever mechanism.

Remind children that they have been working like scientists as they have carried out a fair test to gather data to answer the question and have used the data gathered to make further predictions.

Pupil Workbook: Complete Activity 3: Conclusion on page 15.

Answers

The data shows that as the length of the lever increases, the force required to lift the load decreases.

Homework suggestions

Using a set of data from the enquiry activity during the lesson, children could draw a graph and predict the force required to lift the same load using a lever of 50 cm and 100 cm.

Assessment and evidence of learning

Children can:

- draw a labelled diagram of a lever mechanism
- measure a force, choosing the force meter with the most appropriate scale
- explain why they decided to take a chosen number of repeat readings
- use the data gathered to answer the enquiry question.

Lesson 7: How do gears work?

What children will learn and do

- Children learn that gears are wheels with teeth that can change the direction of movement and the force required to move something.
- They learn that adjacent gears turn in opposite directions, smaller gears turn faster than larger gears, and that a smaller force is needed to turn a smaller gear than a larger gear.
- They investigate plastic gear wheels to find out how they work together in a system.
- They answer the lesson question: **'How do gears work?'**

You will need

- two egg whites
- two bowls
- a balloon whisk
- a rotary whisk
- commercially produced plastic gear wheels (enough for one set of four different-sized gear wheels per pair of children); these gears often have many teeth, so colouring one of the cogs with a contrasting nail polish will help children count the number of revolutions when they start investigating (alternatively, you could make your own gear sets using stiff card circles of different sizes, wooden lollipop sticks, glue and cocktails sticks with blunted ends. There are also good online gear simulations available)
- cork boards or pieces of cardboard, for children to pin their gears to (one per pair)
- digital camera

Snap Science Year 5 Pupil Workbook

- pages 16–17

Snap Science Year 5 Digital subscription

- Slideshow 1: Gears
- Video 1: Cyclist clip
- Snapshot 1: Annotating mechanisms

Make sure you have opened/printed any Snap resources you intend to use in this lesson.

National Curriculum

Conceptual knowledge:

- recognise that some mechanisms, including levers, pulleys and gears, allow a smaller force to have a greater effect

Working scientifically:

- reporting and presenting findings from enquiries, including conclusions, causal relationships [and explanations of and degree of trust in results, in oral and written forms such as displays and other presentations]

Key vocabulary	
Tier 2 vocabulary: anticlockwise, clockwise, system	**Tier 3 vocabulary:** force, gears, lever, load, mechanism, pulley

Health and safety Please refer to CLEAPSS for Health and Safety guidance and ensure that any identified hazards are managed appropriately.

Getting started

Remind children that in the last two lessons they have been learning about mechanisms, which are devices that make it easier to move something. Ask children to discuss with their partner what they have learnt about pulleys and levers. They should recall that as the number of pulleys is increased, the force needed to lift the load is reduced, and that as the length of the lever is increased, the force required to lift the load is reduced.

Ask two children to each whisk an egg white, one using a balloon hand whisk and one using a rotary whisk. Ask them to do this for 30 seconds and then swap whisks. Ask them which whisk was easier to use to beat the egg white and how the machine (the rotary whisk) made it easier.

Explain the following: The rotary whisk has gears. Gears are another simple mechanism. Gears are wheels that have teeth that slot together with the teeth on another gear. When one gear is turned, it turns the gear next to it.

Display Slideshow 1: Gears. Show slide 1, which shows the two whisks and a close-up of the gears on the rotary whisk. Explain that gears make some things easier to do by changing the force needed to make something move. Ask children to discuss how gears are similar and different to pulleys. For example: They are both wheels. A pulley is useful on its own, whereas you always need two gears.

Using the commercial gear set, show the children how to mount two gears onto the board so that the teeth fit together. Demonstrate how turning one gear turns the one next to it. Ask: What have you noticed about the direction each gear is moving? Are they moving at the same speed?

Tell children that they are going to work in pairs to answer the lesson question: **'How do gears work?'**

The task

Give each pair of children commercially produced plastic gears of different sizes – four per pair, plus a board to pin them to.

Ask them to construct different gear systems that use at least three different-sized gears with different numbers of teeth (cogs). They need to make careful observations to count the number of teeth on the different gears and the number of turns, and the changes to the direction of movement that occur when the gears are combined.

Ask children to record the different gear systems they make in labelled diagrams to show which one turns the fastest and with arrows to show the direction of movement.

Pupil Workbook: Complete Activity 1: Constructing gear systems on page 16.

Adaptations and support

Children could photograph their systems and annotate with arrows and speed labels.

Take it further

Children could be encouraged to look for a pattern between the number of teeth on adjacent gears and how quickly they rotate in relation to each other. For example, if there are half as many teeth on the smaller gear, it turns twice for each rotation of the larger gear.

Reflect and review

Remind the children of today's question: **'How do gears work?'**

Show slide 2 of Slideshow 1: Gears and ask the children to think about what they learnt when exploring the gear set. Ask: If gear A turns clockwise, which of the other three gears turn clockwise and which turn anticlockwise? (A and C turn clockwise. B and D turn anticlockwise.) Which gears turn at the same speed? (A and C turn at the same speed.) Which gear turns the fastest? (D.)

Play Video 1: Cyclist clip. Ask children to watch how the speed of the pedalling changes when he is cycling along a flat road, up a hill and in a time trial. Explain to them that increasing the size of one gear, where the pedals are attached, makes the smaller gears on the back wheel turn faster but with less force required.

Show slide 3 of Slideshow 1: Gears. Explain to children that the smaller gear requires less force to make it turn, but it turns much more quickly.

Show slide 4 and ask children to use what they have learnt during the lesson to complete the sentences orally.

Ask children to write today's question: **'How do gears work?'** in their books. They can use the sentence structures on slide 4 to answer the question.

Pupil Workbook: Complete Activity 2: Looking at gears on page 17 and Activity 3: How do gears work? on page 17.

Answers

- If a gear is rotating clockwise, the gear next to it will rotate anticlockwise.
- The smaller the gear, the fewer teeth it has. It rotates faster but requires less force.
- The larger the gear, the more teeth it has. It rotates slower and requires more force.

Homework suggestions

Children could look for objects that contain gears around the home or research other objects that use gears.

Assessment and evidence of learning

Children can use their drawings to:

- explain that gears next to each other rotate in opposite directions
- explain that smaller gears have fewer teeth and rotate more quickly
- explain that a smaller gear requires less force to turn it.

If you are unsure if a child can explain that some mechanisms, including levers, pulleys and gears, allow a smaller force to have a greater effect, you can use Snapshot 1: Annotating mechanisms to check understanding and develop the learning.

Module 2: Properties and uses of materials

Lesson 1: How can we compare and group materials?

What children will learn and do

- Children learn technical vocabulary to accurately describe the properties of a range of materials.
- They distinguish between an object and the material it is made from.
- They identify specific criteria to answer the lesson question: 'How can we compare and group materials?'

You will need

- wooden ruler, metal key and wooden pencil (one set for teacher modelling)
- familiar classroom objects, for example: marker pen, pencil, paper clip, plant pot, sweatshirt, sports shoe, stapler, ruler, water bottle, lunch box, eraser, headband/hair scrunchie (one set per group)
- sticky notes (one packet per group)
- real objects and substances in small containers, for example: milk, jelly, sand, metal key, cooking oil, flour, wooden ruler, sponge, lemonade, aluminium foil, chalk, butter, marshmallow, cork, square of cotton towelling fabric (one set per group)
- beaker of water (one per group)
- magnet (one per group)
- equipment to make a simple circuit: wires, batteries and bulbs (one set per group)
- small tank of water (one per class)
- a sample of each of the following: butter, brick, vegetarian mallow sweet, vegetarian jelly sweet, cheese (such as Edam), cooked pasta, elastic, foil, net (or old tights) and sand (one set per group)
- blunt table knife (one per group)
- a range of weights/masses (one set per group)

If using the Snap Science Year 5 Pupil Workbook you may not require all the resource sheets below.

Snap Science Year 5 Pupil Workbook

- pages 18–20

Snap Science Year 5 Digital subscription

- Resource sheet 1: Comparing materials (one per child)
- Resource sheet 2: Property definition list (one per group as a prompt)
- Resource sheet 3: Compare and contrast grid (one per group to record)
- Resource sheet 4: Hardness comparison grid (one per group to record) (optional)
- Resource sheet 5: Hardness scale (one per group to record) (optional)

Make sure you have opened/printed any *Snap* resources you intend to use in this lesson.

National Curriculum

Conceptual knowledge:

- compare and group together everyday materials on the basis of their properties, including their hardness, [solubility], transparency, conductivity (electrical and thermal), and response to magnets

Working scientifically:

- taking measurements, using a range of scientific equipment, [with increasing accuracy and precision, taking repeat readings when appropriate]
- recording data and results of increasing complexity using [scientific diagrams and labels, classification keys,] tables, [scatter graphs, bar and line graphs]

Key vocabulary	
Tier 2 vocabulary:	Tier 3 vocabulary: comparative test, observe/observation absorb/absorbent, brittle, criterion, durable, ductile, elastic/elasticity, electrical conductor, electrical insulator, flexible, hardness, impermeable, liquid, magnetic, malleable, material, , opaque, permeable, property, rigid, scale, solid, thermal conductor, thermal insulator, translucent, transparent

Health and safety Please refer to CLEAPSS for Health and Safety guidance and ensure that any identified hazards are managed appropriately.

Getting started

Organise children into groups of three or four and give each a selection of familiar classroom objects to observe and discuss. Make sure that there is a good mix of objects made of different materials and with different properties. Check that children know what all the objects are. Ask: What materials are the objects made from? What properties could describe the materials?

Make sure that the distinction is established here between the materials the objects are made from, for example, metal, plastic, and the properties of those materials, for example, hard, shiny. Ask children, in groups, to write the property words that they have come up with on separate sticky notes. Take feedback from children about the properties they have identified. Prompt them to use technical vocabulary to describe properties, for example: absorbent, brittle, durable, ductile, elastic, electrical conductor, electrical insulator, flexible, hard, malleable, transparent, translucent, opaque, permeable/impermeable, rigid, thermal conductor, thermal insulator, magnetic.

Explain to the children that they are going to play 'materials dominoes' in their groups. Model the game yourself first. Place an object where the children can see it. Identify material and property words for that object. For example, for a wooden ruler, the material and property words could be wood and hard respectively. Choose a child who has to select an object to place next to the ruler to match either the property (two points) or material (one point), as with a traditional game of dominoes. For example, the choice to go next to the wooden ruler could be a pencil because it is made of wood or a metal key because it is hard. Ask another child to add an additional object to the 'domino' chain, identifying possible material and property words.

In groups of three or four, the children should then play the game with the objects on their tables by adding objects to either end of the 'domino' chain with the aim of using up all of the objects, keeping score as they play.

Pupil Workbook: Complete Activity 1: Comparing materials on page 18.

The task

In groups of three or four, give children a collection of real materials to handle and explore, and Resource sheet 1: Comparing materials. This includes a list of 16 possible materials. Ask children to use the grid to classify and group their collection. They should begin with solid and liquid as sorting criteria, to establish their baseline understanding of this core knowledge (taught in Year 4). They should then move on to identifying their own criteria to move their learning forward. Ask the lesson question: **'How can we compare and group materials?'**

Be ready to offer prompts to get them started and refer them to Resource sheet 2: Property definition list, if necessary. As they think about the criteria they will choose to compare and sort materials, challenge children to think about less obvious or visible properties, for example, whether the material/s would be waterproof, or a thermal insulator, or magnetic. They can use Resource sheet 3: Compare and contrast grid as a prompt.

Ask: How are the materials similar? How are they different? What property could describe the difference/s? Which properties have you used to sort your materials? Is there a property that is only appropriate to one or two materials? Are any of the materials transparent? Would any conduct electricity?

Pupil Workbook: Complete Activity 2: Classifying properties on page 19.

Adaptations and support

Choose an appropriate selection of materials from the list if you feel 16 is too many for the children to compare.

Take it further

Explain that the task is to compare and contrast objects based upon their hardness. Provide children with a block of butter and a brick to compare. On a hardness scale from 1 to 10 (10 being the hardest), where would butter and a brick be? Then give them additional objects: vegetarian mallow sweets, jelly sweets, cheese (such as Edam), cooked pasta, elastic, foil, net (or old tights) and sand. Ask: Can you identify which solids are harder than brick, softer than butter or anywhere in between? Children should use Resource sheet 4: Hardness comparison grid, to compare the materials the objects are made from. Encourage children to carry out a simple comparative test to establish a rough order of hardness across the materials in the selection. If necessary, model ways in which they might compare the solids, for example, by observing how much they stretch when pulled, or how much they squash when a mass is placed on top of them.

Ask: How can you test these solids to make sure you have put them in the right place on the scale? How soft can a solid be, and still be classified as a solid? Are all solids soft in the same way? What do you mean by the word 'soft' and 'hard' when you are describing a solid?

Children should write a brief description of their methods and what they find out. They should then use the information gathered to complete Resource sheet 5: Hardness scale and order the materials according to hardness.

Pupil Workbook: Complete Activity 3: Comparing solid objects on page 20.

Reflect and review

Ask the lesson question: **'How can we compare and group materials?'** Share responses and consolidate the learning by recording properties of materials listed on the board. Discuss definitions for the following properties: hard, flexible, elastic, brittle, permeable, magnetic, electrical conductor/insulator, thermal insulator/conductor, transparent, opaque, waterproof.

Ask one of the groups of children to share two of the materials that they compared. Ask: How are the two materials you have chosen the same? Which properties do they have in common? How are they different? Repeat with other pairs of children, ensuring they are sharing different materials each time.

Select and show children two objects that are made of the same material in different forms, for example, a metal food tray and a rigid metal object, like the frame of a chair. Again, ask children about the similarities and differences between the materials. Ensure that children recognise that both are solids and both are made of metal, and that they share some properties but also have different properties, for example, a food tray is much less rigid than a chair frame.

For children who have completed the 'Take it further' hardness scale, ask: Could you come up with a definition that might help other children understand that solids can be very different, but are still solids?

Answers

How can we group materials according to their properties?

- flexible: sponge, aluminium foil, cotton fabric, marshmallow
- rigid: metal key, wooden ruler
- malleable: butter, mallow sweet, jelly sweet, sponge, aluminium foil
- transparent: lemonade, steam
- opaque: milk, sand, metal key, flour, wooden ruler, aluminium foil, chalk, butter, marshmallow, cork
- thermal conductor: metal key, cooking oil, aluminium foil
- thermal insulator: flour, sand, sponge, cork, cotton fabric
- permeable: sponge, cork, cotton fabric
- waterproof: metal key, aluminium foil
- electrical conductor: metal key, aluminium foil (cooking oil, milk)
- electrical insulator: wooden ruler, cork, cotton fabric
- magnetic: metal key

How might we compare two materials?

- Comparing two solids: metal key and aluminium foil. Similarities: solid, made from metal, opaque, waterproof, electrical conductors. Differences: a key is rigid and foil is flexible; a key is attracted to a magnet and foil is not.
- Comparing a solid and a liquid: cooking oil and flour. Similarities: oil and flour flow when poured; neither are attracted to a magnet. Differences: oil is a liquid and flour is a solid; oil is transparent and flour is opaque; flour is a thermal insulator and oil is a thermal conductor.

How is the term material used in science? Sometimes we use the word 'material' to describe fabric and textiles. In science the word 'material' is used to describe what something is made of. Some materials have easily observable features, such as transparency, whereas the features of others are less obvious and need to be identified using a range of tests.

Is a solid always hard? 'Soft' solids, like sponge or foam (used in soft furnishings), are still defined as a solid, as are sand and flour, which behave a little like liquids when spilt from a container. The close study of grains under a microscope enables the observation of the grains of sand and the solid structure of each one.

How can we order objects on a scale of hardness from soft (1) to hard (10)? This will depend on temperature and the type of material used but as a general guide the scale might look something like this:

1 butter
2 mallow sweet
3 cooked pasta (depends how al dente it is)
4 cheese (depends on the type of cheese)
5 jelly sweet (depends upon the brand of sweet)
6 net/old tights
7 elastic
8 sand (depends if it is an individual grain or a container full of grains)
9 foil (depends on thickness)
10 brick

Homework suggestions

The next lesson is about materials used in buildings. Ask children to look out for new buildings being built in the locality. Prompt them to make a note about how the buildings are being made and what materials are being used. If there are no new buildings nearby, look at existing buildings or buildings on TV.

Assessment and evidence of learning

Children can:

- identify the difference between an object and the material it is made from
- use technical vocabulary to describe properties accurately
- make comparisons between different materials, identifying their similarities and differences
- use technical vocabulary accurately to describe the properties of materials
- identify specific criteria, based on their understanding of the properties of materials, to compare, sort and create groups
- compare a variety of solid materials according to their properties
- rank a variety of solid materials according to the property of hardness
- describe the different properties of soft solids and hard solids in detail, naming examples and comparing them.

Lesson 2: Which materials did the builders use when constructing our school and why?

What children will learn and do

- Children apply their knowledge about properties of materials to revisit the idea that objects are made from materials with properties that make them fit-for-purpose.
- They learn how materials may vary in form (e.g. plastics of different types) and identify why they are used for particular purposes.
- They conduct a 'wear and tear' survey of materials used in the school building.
- They write a report to communicate their findings from the materials survey.
- They answer the lesson question: **'Which materials did the builders use when constructing our school and why?'**

You will need

- hard hat for teacher (optional)
- high visibility jacket for teacher (optional)
- cameras (one per group)
- photographs of key places in the school building (optional)

If using the Snap Science Year 5 Pupil Workbook you may not require all the resource sheets below.

Snap Science Year 5 Pupil Workbook

- pages 21–23

Snap Science Year 5 Digital subscription

- Video 1: Building construction
- Resource sheet 1: Building surveyor monologue (one for the teacher to read out)
- Resource sheet 2: Materials survey recording grid (one per child or per group)

Make sure you have opened/printed any *Snap* resources you intend to use in this lesson.

National Curriculum

Conceptual knowledge:

- compare and group together everyday materials on the basis of their properties, including their hardness, [solubility], transparency, conductivity (electrical and thermal), and response to magnets
- give reasons, based on evidence from comparative and fair tests, for the particular uses of everyday materials, including metals, wood and plastic

Working scientifically:

- reporting and presenting findings from enquiries, including conclusions, causal relationships and explanations of and a degree of trust in results, in oral and written forms such as displays and other presentations
- about the methods scientists use to build scientific knowledge about materials and how they can be used in different ways
- that scientists make and use observations to answer scientific questions and explain natural phenomena, that they use scientific equipment to quantify their observations and use models to help understand how systems and processes work

Scientific enquiry type:

- identifying and classifying

Key vocabulary	
Tier 2 vocabulary:	**Tier 3 vocabulary:**
construction, structure	observe/observation

	brittle, durable, fragile, property, wear and tear, weathering

Health and safety Please refer to CLEAPSS for Health and Safety guidance and ensure that any identified hazards are managed appropriately.

Getting started

Find out how much exposure children have had to building projects, either through personal experience or through the media. Ask: Have you seen a building being built, perhaps near your home, in the locality, or from watching DIY TV programmes? Discuss responses. If there is a building being completed in the local area, take photographs to show the children to prompt responses.

Ask: What is the first stage of building a building on site? What types of materials are used for buildings? How are buildings constructed? Explain to children that it usually takes many months to construct a building like a house or a school. Plans have to be drawn up, permission given for buildings to be built, a construction team put in place, and materials ordered and brought onto site before construction can start.

Show children Video 1: Materials used in building construction. Ask children to look out for the different construction materials that are being used. How are the materials put together? What are their different purposes? Show the video a second time, so that they can make notes.

Explain that one of the professions involved when a building is constructed is a building surveyor. Put on a hard hat and/or a high visibility jacket and go into the role as a building surveyor. Read out Resource sheet 1: Building surveyor monologue. Ask: What does a building surveyor do? What science is involved in this role?

Pupil Workbook: Complete Activity 1: What do building surveyors do? on page 21.

The task

Explain that the children are going to be in-role as a building surveyor. Their task is to carry out an identification and classification enquiry to answer the lesson question: **'Which materials did the builders use when constructing our school and why?'** They will survey the materials used in the school building (inside and outside if appropriate). Their focus will be on observing the wear and tear and weathering of the materials used in the building. Establish the difference between objects which are in the building (e.g. tables, chairs, cupboards) and materials that form the structure of the building (e.g. ceiling tiles, door frames, windows, electrical cables). Children will focus on the latter. Ask: What do we mean by wear and tear to a material? What do we mean by weathering? What signs of wear and tear, to the materials around school, might you see? They will be looking for and recording five things:

1 Identifying the uses of different types of materials and their location around school.
2 Consider why the materials have been chosen. What properties do the materials that the building parts are made from have? What properties make them fit for purpose?
3 What signs of wear and tear or weathering to the materials are there? What were/are the potential causes of the wear and tear or weathering. (For example: exposure to extreme weather or regular use over time.)
4 Is the material still fit-for-purpose? What properties might be used for worn materials? Brittle or fragile? Is the material durable?
5 Is any action required to repair or replace the material?

Ask: What properties of materials might you observe used on the building: hard; durable; ductile; flexible; strong; elastic; smooth; flexible; transparent/translucent/opaque; electrical conductors/insulators; thermal conductors/insulators; magnetic; absorbent/waterproof.

Ask: How are you going to measure and record the wear and tear? Discuss possible solutions. Put children in groups of 2–3 to devise their own scale/system. Use an example from your school building to model how to conduct the survey. For example:

1 vinyl floor tiles used on the classroom floor
2 material is durable, opaque, hard, waterproof and may be a thermal insulator
3 worn floor tiles by the classroom door threshold could be caused by the repeated opening/closing of the classroom door and the tread from frequent foot traffic
4 some scratches rated at 3/10 (1 meaning showing least sign of wear and tear and 10 meaning completely worn/broken/no longer fit-for-purpose)
5 tiles do not need to be replaced now but should be monitored for further wear and tear in six months.

In their groups, children should note their observations and ideas in a jotter or use Resource sheet 3: Materials survey recording grid. They should be encouraged to take photographic evidence. On return to the classroom give children some time to organise the data that they have collected, identifying where the most significant evidence of wear and tear and weathering was seen. Ask: What do you think is the cause of the wear and tear you have observed? How could you find out more about the causes of damage to the materials around our school? Ask: Which materials are manufactured and which materials are natural. Is there a difference to the ways these materials wear or are weathered?

Tell children to produce a report for the headteacher using either an annotated plan of the school building or a sequence of annotated photographs to show their findings and suggest improvements where appropriate.

Pupil Workbook: Complete Activity 2: Surveying your school on page 22 and Activity 3: Writing a report on page 23.

Adaptations and support

Give children a short list of key places to visit in the school (using photographs as visual prompts) that have various signs of wear and tear. At the location children can be supported to identify the materials using a materials/properties vocabulary list.

Take it further

Explain that it is important to have very good insulation in and around our schools. Not only does good insulation make everyone's time in school more comfortable, but it can also reduce the enormous cost of heating the buildings and help reduce energy wastage. Ask: Where do you think we lose most heat from our school buildings? Children should complete some research using secondary sources into how buildings can have improved insulation. Ask: What types of materials are often used to insulate buildings? What particular properties do these materials have in common that makes them suitable to use?

Children then survey the building to identify where insulation could be safely improved, recording the evidence that they collect, producing either an annotated plan of the school building or a sequence of annotated photographs to show where insulation could be improved, suggesting appropriate materials from their research.

Reflect and review

Encourage children to discuss in their groups the answer to the lesson question: **'Which materials did the builders use when constructing our school and why?'** Discuss as a whole class to draw out the properties of different materials used around the school to ensure comprehensive coverage of all properties: hard; durable; ductile; flexible; strong; elastic; smooth; flexible; transparent/translucent/opaque; electrical conductors/insulators; thermal conductors/insulators; magnetic; absorbent/waterproof. Ask: What type of scientific enquiry do we use to answer the question? Confirm that the children identified the material and classified them by their properties and the way they have changed over time through wear and tear and weathering.

As a class, debate the five most worn and weathered areas that require attention around the school and develop a top five list of materials that need to be replaced. Ask: Do you need any further information or evidence from additional research?

Answers

Why have certain materials been used in the structure of the building?

- asphalt roof: flexible, durable, waterproof, smooth
- blinds/curtains: opaque, flexible, durable, thermal insulators
- bricks: strong, durable, reasonably waterproof
- cavity wall insulation: thermal insulator
- classroom ceiling tiles: thermal insulator, opaque,
- double glazing: the vacuum in between the layers of glass reduces the thermal conduction of heat
- drainpipe: waterproof, strong, durable
- flooring around play equipment: malleable, flexible, elastic, permeable
- glass windows: transparent, solid, durable, smooth
- metal door handle: strong, smooth, waterproof
- metal taps: strong, waterproof, durable
- plastic light switch/socket: electrical insulator, waterproof, durable
- slate roof: hard, durable, waterproof, smooth
- tiles behind sink in toilet: waterproof, durable, smooth
- vinyl flooring: hard, flexible, waterproof, smooth
- wooden door: solid, hard wearing, when painted/varnished – waterproof

What is meant by the term: 'wear and tear'?

Materials used in building construction, although selected for use because of their durability, will show signs of wear and tear over time. Wear and tear is the damage that happens to a material through ordinary regular use (or abuse) over a period of time. Examples include: scuff marks on tiled floor; handles on a door becoming wobbly as screws are worked loose due to the vibrations caused by repeatedly slamming the door closed; a carpet becoming threadbare or soiled from frequent foot traffic.

What is meant by the term: 'weathered'?

Materials may change colour or the surface may deteriorate over a period of time because of the effects of rain, sun, wind or other weather conditions. Examples include: varnish or paint on an external door becoming weathered and worn away by rain and wind; roof tiles becoming covered in lichen or moss or broken when hit by large hailstones; paint on painted window sills blistering when overheating on hot days and cracking in below-zero temperatures.

What happens to certain materials when they are weathered or worn?

Many metals, unless protected by paint or treated in another way, will start to oxidise, forming rust. Many organic materials, for example wood, will decompose once the surface seal or varnish is broken. Plastics start to break down and can become brittle.

Where could insulation be improved around the school?

Double or triple glazing; reflective glass; thick ceiling/roof insulation (using environmentally friendly materials such as reclaimed wool); underfloor insulation; cavity wall-insulation; effective seals around door and windows for draught proofing, insulation around water tanks and water pipe; installing porches or vestibules.

Other ways to save energy, to complement the insulation, might include: heat reclamation systems, solar power panels on the roof; wind turbines.

Homework suggestions

Ask: Can you design a home that would be really well insulated and made from environmentally friendly materials and renewable resources? How would you stop heat escaping from your home? What features would you include? What would the building surveyor say when he visited to inspect your home?

Assessment and evidence of learning

Children can:

- identify a wide variety of different materials used around school, describing how materials may vary in form and identifying why they are used for certain jobs
- identify the properties of materials used for the different purposes in the structure of the building
- give examples of where certain materials are showing signs of decay, wear or weathering and suggest potential reasons
- make judgements about the materials being fit for purpose
- create a scale to rate the severity of wear and/or weathering
- identify key points to feed back within a report to the head teacher, as part of their building survey.

Lesson 3: Which liquid is the thickest?

What children will learn and do

- Children learn about the viscosity of different liquids.
- They create a concept map to show the difference between solids that behave like liquids and liquids themselves.
- They carry out a comparative test, exploring the viscosity of different liquids.
- They answer the lesson question: **'Which liquid is the thickest?'**

You will need

- different coloured pens (one packet per group)
- sheet of A2 paper (one per group)
- glue stick (one per group)
- liquids: honey, cooking oil, syrup, milk, washing up liquid, bubble bath, lemonade, yoghurt (one set per group)
- wipe-clean ramps, mini whiteboards (one per group)
- measuring spoons/teaspoons/tablespoons (one per group)
- a means of cleaning and drying the spoons (one set per group)
- stop watches or watches with second hands (one per group)
- a range of empty measuring containers/beakers for pouring into (one set per group)
- rulers (one per group)
- different brands of tomato ketchup (one set of various ketchups per group)
- shallow tray, cornflour, spoon, water (for teacher modelling)

If using the Snap Science Year 5 Pupil Workbook you may not require all the resource sheets below.

Snap Science Year 5 Pupil Workbook

- pages 24–26

Snap Science Year 5 Digital subscription

- Resource sheet 1: Concept word cards (one set of cards per group)
- Resource sheet 2: Graph template (one per child)

Make sure you have opened/printed any *Snap* resources you intend to use in this lesson.

National Curriculum

Conceptual knowledge:

- compare and group together everyday materials on the basis of their properties, [including their hardness, solubility, transparency, conductivity (electrical and thermal), and response to magnets]
- give reasons, based on evidence from comparative and fair tests, for the particular uses of everyday materials, [including metals, wood and plastic]

Working scientifically:

- planning different types of scientific enquiries to answer questions, including recognising and controlling variables where necessary
- taking measurements, using a range of scientific equipment, with increasing accuracy and precision, taking repeat readings when appropriate
- recording data and results of increasing complexity using scientific diagrams and labels, [classification keys, tables, scatter graphs,] bar and line graphs
- reporting and presenting findings from enquiries, including conclusions, causal relationships and explanations of and a degree of trust in results, in oral and written forms such as displays and other presentations

Scientific enquiry type:

- comparative [and fair] testing

Key vocabulary	
Tier 2 vocabulary: flow, pour	**Tier 3 vocabulary:** comparative test liquid, property, solid, viscosity/viscous

Health and safety Please refer to CLEAPSS for Health and Safety guidance and ensure that any identified hazards are managed appropriately.

Getting started

Ask: What is a liquid? Give each table of children a set of Resource sheet 1: Concept word cards, together with a large sheet of paper and pens. Explain that they are going to create a concept map together using these words, linking the words with arrows and labelling the links to show the connections. Model this process using two or three of the concept words, adding links and **defining** the link to show how a concept map is created. For example, washing up liquid and oil are both linked to 'container'; on the line between the words add the link phrase 'can be held in'. Tell them that every child should add to the map. Once completed, each child's contributions can be identified (and assessed) by the different coloured pen used by each child.

Check that all children have a clear understanding of the **difference** between the solids that behave like liquids **(salt and sand)** and liquids themselves.

Pupil Workbook: Complete Activity 1: Solid or liquid? on page 24.

The task

Tell children that the lesson question is: **'Which liquid is the thickest?'** Ask: How would you describe a liquid? Are all liquids the same? Ask: Do all liquids flow? Can all liquids be poured?

Ensure that children identify relative thickness as one of the ways in which liquids differ. Introduce the terms viscous (**thick**) and viscosity (how thick something is) as a property. Explain that during this lesson they are going to be finding out about the viscosity of liquids. They will be planning and carrying out a comparative test enquiry to find out which is the **thickest** liquid, including identifying a method, setting up equipment, and recording what they find. In groups they discuss possible test methods they might use.

Encourage children to think of ways in which they could find out an answer to the question: Which is the thickest liquid? Which is the **thinnest** liquid? If necessary, prompt them by offering a selection of containers with different liquids that they might test. They could shake to listen and look at how the liquids move in their containers. After a few minutes, discuss possible test approaches as a whole class.

Remind children that they will need to plan how they will set up their **comparative test** and decide on the equipment they will use and what evidence they will collect. Tell them to record their results in a bar chart using **Resource sheet 2: Graph template** and label the axes with the different types of liquid (horizontal axis) and time taken (vertical axis).

After they have completed their enquiry, ask them to order the liquids from thinnest to thickest. Ask: How do we know which of these is the thickest? How could you measure the thickness of each liquid more accurately? Can you think of any other thick liquids we could have tested? Where would they fit into the order? Children then annotate their bar chart with the answers to these questions.

Pupil Workbook: Complete Activity 2: Comparative test enquiry: viscosity of liquids on page 24 and Activity 3: Results on page 26.

Adaptations and support

Ensure children have the opportunity for hands-on experience of the different liquids in their containers before planning their test. Reduce the number of liquids tested. Alternatively organise the test as a carousel activity, placing a different liquid on each table and asking the groups to move around as they test them.

Take it further

Children plan a comparative test to find out if different brands of tomato ketchup are similar in thickness. Ask: Are all ketchups the same? How are they different? How does their thickness vary? Do thicker ketchups contain the most tomatoes? Are the thicker ketchups the most expensive? Why? Are some brands of ketchup redder than others? Why?

Encourage children to discuss possible questions related to the viscosity of the ketchups and then decide which one they would like to investigate. They should decide on a method, what equipment to use, what evidence to collect, where they might look for that evidence and how to record it.

Reflect and review

Ask some children to describe to the class the comparative test they carried out and what they found out about the viscosity of liquids. Ask the lesson question: **'Which liquid is the thickest?'** Discuss as a class. Ask: Which of the liquids were the thickest? Were there any surprises? Why?

Ask those children that completed the tomato ketchup task: What were the differences between the thickness of the ketchups you looked at? Did any of the ketchups include 'thickeners' in the ingredients? Explain that this may mean they include cornflour, which is a thickener, or a similar material in their ingredients.

For the ketchup group, you may decide to complete the following:

Explain that cornflour is a common thickener. Show children what happens to water when cornflour is added. Sprinkle some cornflour onto a large tray. Gradually add water to the cornflour, stirring it slowly to combine the two. Ask: What do you notice happens when the mixture is stirred slowly? What happens when it is stirred quickly? Can you scoop some of the mixture out and roll it into a ball? What happens when you stop rolling it? What seems to make the cornflour suddenly harden?

Explain that it is the movement of the cornflour and water mixture as it is stirred that causes it to stiffen. Use the observations about the behaviour of cornflour and water to encourage children to think again about the viscosity of tomato ketchup. Ask: What do you think would happen if cornflour were added to tomato ketchup? Would the liquid ketchup become thicker? Or thinner? What do you think would happen if the ketchup were shaken up (which we often do to make it easier to pour)?

Answers

What is a liquid?

Liquids when poured from place to place take the shape of the container they are in but do not change in volume. The surface of a liquid will remain horizontal when the container is tipped. Liquids cannot be compressed.

What is viscosity?

Viscosity is the property of a liquid that describes how fast or slowly it will flow. This is also referred to as how thick or thin a liquid is. A thick liquid, like Greek style yoghurt, is said to have a high viscosity, and will flow slowly. A thin liquid, like water, is said to have low viscosity, and will flow quickly.

What tests could children conduct?

- timing how long it takes for a liquid to pour from an unshaken bottle or from a large spoon, or timing how long after pouring it takes for a quantity of liquid to form a flat surface.
- a trickle test, timing how long it takes for a small amount of the liquid to travel down a slope from a fixed height. The one that takes the longest to trickle down will be the thickest.

Why are thickeners used in some brands of tomato ketchup?

Thickeners are sometimes used in cheap ketchups. More expensive tomato ketchups tend to be thicker because they include large quantities of tomatoes. These products thin when shaken, rather than thicken.

Homework suggestions

Children could research a recipe for eco-friendly slime. They may be able to make this with an adult at home. Ask: Can they make their slime more viscous and/or less viscous?

Assessment and evidence of learning

Children can:

- show their understanding of the properties of liquids
- demonstrate a clear understanding of the difference between solids that behave like liquids and liquids themselves
- independently plan a test to compare the viscosity of liquids
- identify which variables need to be kept the same
- carry out their test using equipment
- measure accurately, using the equipment correctly
- sequence a variety of liquids according to how thick or thin they are
- describe how viscosity varies from liquid to liquid
- accurately record the evidence generated in a bar chart
- label their chart correctly with the variables on the correct axis
- choose a suitable scale with equal intervals and the bars/line drawn correctly
- add annotations which interpret their findings and draw accurate conclusions.

Lesson 4: Who invents things?

What children will learn and do

- Children learn more about how inventors use materials in new ways.
- They invent a new object made of a material that is fit for purpose based upon its properties.
- They think of unusual and creative uses for simple objects made from everyday materials.
- They promote and evaluate their inventions.
- They answer the lesson question: **'How do inventors work?'**

You may choose to split this lesson in two, giving children a good length of time, over a few days or the weekend, to contemplate and come up with an invention. Tell them that some of the best inventors can take years to come up with a great new idea.

You will need

- three paper clips (one in original state to show and use to hold up fabric, one open so that it can be used to open an envelope, one bent into a shape to support a smartphone)
- one piece of fabric
- one envelope
- one smartphone
- wooden chopsticks (one per pair of children)
- paper cup (one per pair of children)
- squares of repurposed waterproof fabric 40 cm x 40 cm (one per pair of children) (N.B. source fabric from old waterproof coats, from unclaimed lost property or a charity shop.)
- 30 cm rulers (one per pair of children)

If using the Snap Science Year 5 Pupil Workbook you may not require the resource sheet below.

Snap Science Year 5 Pupil Workbook

- pages 27–29

Snap Science Year 5 Digital subscription

- Slideshow 1: Bei Ning Koh
- Slideshow 2: Uses of a paper clip
- Resource sheet 1: Inventor's notebook (one per child)
- Snapshot 1: Which materials are suitable?

Make sure you have opened/printed any *Snap* resources you intend to use in this lesson.

National Curriculum

Conceptual knowledge:

- identify and compare the suitability of a variety of everyday materials, including wood, metal, plastic, glass, brick, rock, paper and cardboard, for particular uses

Working scientifically:

- using their observations and ideas to suggest answers to questions

Key vocabulary	
Tier 2 vocabulary: design, invent	**Tier 3 vocabulary:** flexible, property

Health and safety Please refer to CLEAPSS for Health and Safety guidance and ensure that any identified hazards are managed appropriately.

Getting started

Begin by asking the lesson question: **'How do inventors work?'** Ask children what they know about what inventors do. Explain that inventors use science to design and test objects that are new and have not been made before. Ask: Do you know of any amazing inventions? Who invented them?

Using Slideshow 1: Bei Ning Koh, introduce the inventor Bei Ning Koh (Resource 1). Go through the slides one by one reading each speech bubble in turn to tell children about her invention and how she designed it. Ask what properties of the materials used are vital to the success of her design? Note with children that Bei Ning Koh came up with lots of ideas and kept improving her design over and over again.

Show children a paper clip. Ask: What is for? What is it made of? What else could you do with it? Take their ideas and then display Slideshow 2, which shows a number of creative uses for a paper clip. Model these uses in a series of demonstrations. Discuss its properties: flexible – to bend into a new shape to create a smart phone mount; hard and strong – to hold the fabric up on the leg of a pair of trousers; sharp – to open an envelope.

Pupil Workbook: Complete Activity 1: Thinking creatively on page 27.

The task

Explain to children that now it is their chance to use their scientific knowledge and skills and be inventors. Their challenge is to think of new uses for a simple object based on the properties of the material that it is made of and the shape it has been made into. Explain that they should then promote their 'invention' in a television advertisement.

Children work in pairs or individually. Allow them to choose either a paper cup, a wooden chopstick or a piece of waterproof fabric. Encourage them to be as creative as possible, but they must remember to think about the properties of the materials that their object is made from.

The starting point is for the children to produce a thought shower in Resource sheet 1: Inventor's notebook. They create a drawing of the object in the centre. They should answer the questions on the first page: What material is it made from? What properties does the material have?; What shape has the material been made into?; What is the size of the object?; What is the object's purpose?; What is the object used for?; Why and how is the material the object is made from fit for purpose?

Next children need to consider what else could the object be used for. Ask: What can they invent using this object? What if the object were ten times bigger or smaller? What if there were 100 of them? Also encourage children to think about the size and shape of their inventions.

The next stage is to create an ideas board in Resource sheet 1: Inventor's notebook with multiple ideas, just like the paper clips example in Slideshow 2. Discuss the idea that all thoughts should be recorded. One idea may trigger another even better one. Remind them that inventors embrace failures as they can lead to success.

Children then decide on one design and create an annotated drawing in their Inventors notebook detailing and describing their design. They then plan and act out a television advertisement to promote their invention. Explain to them that they should name their invention and think of a slogan to promote it. They should include a demonstration of the invention being used and an explanation of why it is a good idea, how it works, referring to the properties of the material it is made from and how it will improve lives.

Ask children to act out their advertisements.

Then explain that they should choose another child's invention and review it for its: usefulness; inventiveness; use of the material and shape, noting their findings on the last page of Resource sheet 1: Inventor's notebook.

Pupil Workbook: Complete Activity 2: Design your own invention on page 28 and Activity 3: My final design on page 29.

Adaptations and support

Some children may require prompts and support to come up with ideas. Work through the process with them. For example if they were choosing the waterproof fabric, discuss the properties of the fabric. Note that it is flexible and waterproof. Demonstrate how it can be repurposed and made into a baby's bib. This would be a new design and a new use.

Take it further

Some children may want to create a design for a brand-new object that has not yet been invented yet, without using the paper cup, chopstick or waterproof fabric as a starting point. They may choose to use another object/material to inspire their design. They may even decide to invent a new material. They can still use the same structure for the design process and the advertisement.

Reflect and review

Ask the lesson question: **'How do inventors work?'** Discuss responses. Together, create a definition that describes what an inventor does, including reference to science knowledge. Acknowledge that all of the children can be inventors and that the task they completed in the lesson proves that they have the skills and scientific knowledge required to invent new objects or materials. Note that new objects and materials are invented regularly.

Ask some of the children to share their inventions and ask the other children to identify the properties of the materials that make the new designs fit for purpose.

Answers

What is an invention?

An invention is something that someone makes that has not been made before, to serve a particular purpose, using materials in a way not used before.

What did Bei Ning Koh invent?

Bei Ning Koh invented an itch reliever for people who suffer from eczema. Her design includes a metal ball with a raised texture on its surface. This can be rolled over inflamed and irritated skin. The stainless-steel ball feels cooler than the skin, even at room temperature. It is also hard so the pressure, when pressed on the skin, relieves the itch. The rolling mechanism ensures the skin is not scratched as this would cause the eczema to worsen.

What are the properties of the paper clip which make it fit for purpose within a design?

A paper clip is: thin and flexible to be bent into any shape; rigid to keep the fabric, money, keys and bread wrapper in place; strong to hold the weight of a fish; sharp to tear paper and open a letter; lightweight to hang an ornament.

What are the properties of the paper cup which make it fit for purpose within a design?

It is: lightweight, recyclable, holds its shape, able to hold materials and is a thermal insulator. Possible uses: small bag with string attached; rain gauge; decorated paper hat with elastic attached; bird feeder.

What are the properties of the wooden chopstick which make it fit for purpose within a design?

It is: environmentally friendly, light, rigid and lightweight. Possible uses: measuring stick, scratching device, olive pitter, stirrer, shoe/mud scraper.

What are the properties of the repurposed waterproof fabric which make it fit for purpose within a design?

It is: flexible, durable, waterproof and strong. Possible uses: covering for leftover food, book bag, hair scarf, gift wrap, toiletries bag, baby's bib, snack/lunch bag.

Homework suggestions

Set children the task of finding an everyday object at home and thinking of ways it could be used for a new purpose based upon its properties. Note they should complete any exploration with a responsible adult for safety reasons.

Assessment and evidence of learning

Children can:

- describe what an inventor does
- recognise that inventors use scientific knowledge
- understand that the invention process takes time and success can follow failure
- clearly articulate their understanding of the difference between an object and the material it is made from
- use technical vocabulary to describe properties of a material
- accurately explain how these properties make it suitable for its use in an object, referring to material and shape
- make comparisons between materials referring to their properties
- think of new uses for an everyday object
- create a clear annotated design
- review another child's design based upon given criteria
- refer to the properties of the material it is made from
- demonstrate and explain why and how it is fit for purpose.

If you are unsure if a child can identify and compare the suitability of a variety of everyday materials, including wood, metal, plastic, glass, brick, rock, paper and cardboard, for particular use you can use Snapshot 1: Which materials are suitable? to assess understanding and develop learning.

Lesson 5: Can the same container keep cold things cold and hot things hot?

What children will learn and do

- Children observe the disassembly of a cool bag and identify the properties of the materials used in each layer.
- They plan and carry out a comparative test to explore the properties of thermal insulators and their effect on cold and hot food.
- They collect data by taking repeat readings of temperature.
- They present multiple sets of data in a line graph.
- They use their graph to answer questions about temperature change and explain that insulation can keep hot things hot and cold things cold.
- They answer the lesson question: **'Can the same material keep cold things cold and hot things hot?'**

You will need

Model for the children how to be mindful of wasting materials and sending too much waste to landfill. Reuse materials where possible. Insulated lunch bags can be bought cheaply and should be kept to use again in following years, including the one that is disassembled in this lesson. Alternatively children could be asked to bring insulated lunch bags from home to use. You will need to match up then up so that each group has two bags which are the same.

- cool bag (insulated lunch bag) (one for teacher modelling – you will need to take it apart)
- scissors
- tray (one for teacher)
- ice lollies (in paper not plastic) or ice cubes , should weigh about 150 – 200 g) (two of each per group)
- baked jacket potatoes, which should weigh 150 – 200 g), cooled slightly after baking, (two per group) or you can use hot water (maximum temperature – 50°C, 150-200ml) (two of each per group)
- (Note if using water and ice cubes you will need to be careful that they don't spill in the cool bag.)
- containers to put ice lolly and potato/water in on table (two per group)
- data loggers with temperature probes or thermometers (minimum one per group - ideally six per group)
- timers (count up) (one per group)
- cool bags (two identical per group)
- materials (selection of samples of fabric large enough to wrap the containers: cotton fabric, woollen fabric, polyester/synthetic fabric, bubble wrap, paper, cotton wool, aluminium foil)
- scissors (as required)
- tape (as required)
- string (as required)
- elastic bands (as required)

If using the Snap Science Year 5 Pupil Workbook you may not require all the resource sheets below.

Snap Science Year 5 Pupil Workbook

- pages 30–33

Snap Science Year 5 Digital subscription

- Slideshow 1: Cool bag ideas
- Resource sheet 1: Results table (one per child or group) (optional)
- Resource sheet 2: Graph template for cool bag test (one per child) (optional)

Make sure you have opened/printed any *Snap* resources you intend to use in this lesson.

National Curriculum

Conceptual knowledge:

- compare and group together everyday materials on the basis of their properties, including their [hardness, solubility, transparency,] conductivity (electrical and thermal), [and response to magnets]
- give reasons, based on evidence from comparative and fair tests, for the particular uses of everyday materials, including metals, wood and plastic

Working scientifically:

- planning different types of scientific enquiries to answer questions, including recognising and controlling variables where necessary
- taking measurements, using a range of scientific equipment, with increasing accuracy and precision, taking repeat readings when appropriate
- recording data and results of increasing complexity using scientific diagrams and labels, classification keys, tables, scatter graphs, bar and line graphs
- reporting and presenting findings from enquiries, including conclusions, causal relationships and explanations of and a degree of trust in results, in oral and written forms such as displays and other presentations
- identifying scientific evidence that has been used to support or refute ideas or arguments

Scientific enquiry type: comparative testing

Key vocabulary	
Tier 2 vocabulary:	**Tier 3 vocabulary:**
disassemble, heat	comparative test, control variable, data, predict/prediction, variable property, thermal conductor, thermal insulator

Health and safety Please refer to CLEAPSS for Health and Safety guidance and ensure that any identified hazards are managed appropriately.

Getting started

Explain to the class that some people are going on a picnic and the menu that they have decided on includes both ice lollies and hot jacket potatoes! They need to keep the ice lolly in its frozen, solid form and the jacket potato hot for a few hours while they travel to the picnic site. Ask: What do people use when they want to keep food hot or cold? Show the children a cool bag. Ask: Who has had experience of using a cool bag? Did it keep materials hot or cold? Allow children to share experiences.

Tell the class that the people planning the picnic want to know whether the same type of cool bag could be used to keep the jacket potato hot and ice lolly cold. Can we help them by carrying out a test to answer the lesson question: **Can the same material keep cold things cold and hot things hot?**

Disassemble the cool bag in front of the children to show them the various layers. Ask: What do you think each layer is made from? Why do you think the manufacturer chose these materials? What properties do they have? Leave these layers accessible for children to have hands-on experience of the layers during the lesson. Display Slideshow 1: Cool bag ideas. Ask children which of the statements they agree with and how they might test their ideas.

Pupil Workbook: Complete Activity 1: Cool bags on page 30.

The task

In groups of four to six, children will plan a comparative test enquiry to find out how a cool bag affects both hot and cold food. They will use thermometers or data loggers with temperature probes to measure the changes in temperature of a hot jacket potato and frozen ice lolly that are placed in separate but identical cool bags. An additional container with the potato and another container with the ice lolly will be left on a table at room temperature (as controls). Hot water and ice cubes/crushed ice can be used instead, to represent the potato and ice lolly. Ask each group to plan out how they will set up their test and which variables they will need to control.

Discuss how often they will measure the temperature of the ice lolly and the jacket potato. Suggest at one minute, two minutes, five minutes, then every five minutes for 30 minutes. They should decide who in their group is going to measure the temperature of the ice lolly and who is going to measure the temperature of the potato. Ask: What is the best way of taking the temperature of the potato and ice lolly? Explain that the thermometer should be positioned in the potato or ice lolly, so that it can be read by children, without touching the potato. Talk with children about the potential effect of repeatedly opening the bag. Tell them to design a results table to record their data. Before the test begins (and before they are given the potato and ice lollies) each child should draw a labelled diagram of the two potatoes (one in a cool bag and one on a table) and two ice lollies (one in a cool bag and one on a table), to predict what they think will happen.

Children carry out their test and collect the temperature readings. They then draw a line graph to present the data. (The use of Resource sheet 2: Graph template for cool bag test is optional.) There will be four lines on the graph: one for each set of control variable data (potato and ice lolly in the open room) and one for the data for each container of food kept in the two cool bags. Model labelling the axes: time taken (horizontal axis) and temperature (vertical axis) and adding a key to denote which line represents which container/food combination.

Ask: What do the line graphs show about the impact of the cool bag on the temperature of the potato? Tell children to revisit their initial annotated drawing, where they made their prediction, and add further annotations in a different colour presenting their results. Add a simple conclusion. They should be able to state whether a cool bag is better at keeping something cold or hot, or whether there is no difference.

Pupil Workbook: Complete Activity 2: Comparative test enquiry: how do cool bags affect hot and cold food? on page 31, Activity 3: Results table on page 32 and Activity 4: Results bar graph on page 32.

Adaptations and support

Allow children to focus on comparing a potato in a cool bag and a potato on the table to make a simple comparison. Ask: How quickly do you think the potato will cool? Which potato will cool faster? What difference do you think the cool bag will make to the temperature of the potato? Children can record their results on Resource sheet 1: Results table. They can then use Resource sheet 2: Graph template for cool bag test (pre labelled) to create a simple line graph or record a simple voice note/video explaining what happened to the temperature of each container of potato.

Take it further

Children design and carry out a comparative test to see which materials are the best thermal insulators. Then, armed with the data they have collected, they design a four layer picnic bag of their own. They should be prompted to consider other properties of materials (waterproof, flexible, durable) for various layers of the bag. Provide them with large sheets of paper on which to draw and annotate their designs. Remind the children that their design needs to include details of the materials they use (and their properties), the type of insulation they include and how this is arranged in the cool bag. They then make a prototype of their bag and carry out a 'beat the cool bag' comparative test to see if their picnic bag is a better thermal insulator than the commercially available cool bag.

Reflect and review

Ask the lesson question: **'Can the same material keep cold things cold and hot things hot?** Ask: Does your evidence suggest that it should be possible? Did the cool bags you used in your comparative test enquiry work for hot and for cold things? What happened to the temperatures you recorded over time?

Can you explain how a cool bag can keep cold things cold and hot things hot? What do others in the class think?

Allow children to share their conclusions. Give children time to talk with a partner and to come up with a conclusion that summarises what they found out. Ensure that their statements explain that the temperature of the hot foods went down (whether inside or outside the cool bags), while the temperature of the cold foods went up, but that the temperature changed more slowly for those items that were inside the cool bag. Make the point that this happens because the bag is made up of layers of materials which are **thermal insulators**. Discuss the terms thermal insulators: materials that don't transmit heat well. Tell the children that the opposite of a thermal insulator is a thermal conductor which transmits heat very well. Metals are thermal conductors- that is why they are used to make saucepans so that the food inside gets hot quickly. Ask: why do you think that saucepans don't have metal handles? Note the difference between **the terms electrical conductors and electrical insulators** to help avoid any confusion.

Return to the disassembled cool bag. Ask: which layers are likely to be thermal insulators? Are their other properties that make some of the layers fit for purpose when used here? Prompt, flexible, durable and waterproof if necessary.

Ask: Because we have discovered that the same material can keep cold things cold and hot things hot, is the name cool bag appropriate? What alternative names could we use?

Ask children who have completed the 'Take it further' activity to share the designs for their picnic bags. They should explain how particular design features they have included are intended to work.

Answers

What is temperature?

Temperature is a measurement of heat and is measured in degrees Celsius.

How can we make accurate comparisons?

Comparisons to be made:

- between the potato in the cool bag and the potato on the table (acting as a control, outside the cool bag)
- between the ice lolly in the cool bag and the ice lolly on the table (acting as a control, outside the cool bag)
- between the ice lolly in the cool bag and the potato in the cool bag

It is important that certain variables are the same, in order to make valid comparisons. Variables to keep the same:

- weight of the potato and the weight of the ice lolly (roughly)
- temperature of two potatoes to be the same at the beginning of the test – exact
- temperature of two ice lollies to be the same at the beginning of the test – exact
- same type of cool bags

What is a thermal insulator?

A thermal insulator is a material that provides high resistance to heat flow.

Why don't metal saucepans have metal handles?

Metal is a thermal conductor and the handles would get too hot to hold and burn our hands.

What will happen to the potato and the ice lolly in the cool bags?

The temperature of the hot foods will go down (whether inside or outside the cool bags). The temperature of the cold foods will go up. The temperature of the foods in the cool bags will change more slowly than the temperature of those on the table. This is because the bag is made up of layers of materials which are thermal insulators.

What happens to food surrounded by a thermal insulator (in this instance the cool bag)?

A thermal insulator does not allow heat to travel through readily. With the potato in the cool bag, this heat is trapped inside the bag and does not move to the outside air so easily. With the ice lolly in the cool bag, the warmer outside air cannot travel through the bag into the inside of the bag so the inside of the bag remains cool.

Homework suggestions

Ask children to safely observe and record examples of thermal insulators and conductors that they encounter outside of school. Set them a challenge to draw a diagram of an example of a thermal insulator that they think no other child will find. Create a class montage display and use it as a discussion prompt.

Assessment and evidence of learning

Children can:

- apply their knowledge of properties of materials
- offer suggestions why different materials were selected to make the separate layers
- plan a test to see if the same container can keep cold things cold and hot things hot
- identify which variables need to be kept the same
- choose suitable intervals to take temperature readings
- make predictions about what they think will happen giving reasons using an annotated diagram
- carry out their test in an orderly way
- measure accurately, using the thermometer or data logger accurately
- record their results accurately
- plot their results on a line graph
- calculate the change in temperature over time
- write a conclusion which reflects upon the thinking shared in their prediction
- explain how the insulation material in a cool bag helps to keep hot things hot and cool things cool.

Lesson 6: Which materials are absorbent, permeable or waterproof?

Note this lesson has two parts and so needs a longer time than usual, or to be split into two lessons.

What children will learn and do

- Children consider the purpose, functionality and properties of a nappy.
- They observe a disassembly of a disposable nappy to explore the properties of the different layers: absorbent, permeable and waterproof.
- They carry out an enquiry to identify whether the different types of nappy are easy to use, comfortable, flexible, elastic, absorbent, leak proof and waterproof.
- They explore the environmental impact of the manufacture, use and disposal of different types of nappy.
- They answer the lesson question: **'Which is the best type of nappy?'**

You will need (part 1)

- disposable nappy (one to disassemble for teacher modelling) (one nappy per five children to pass around the class)
- A4 tray (one for teacher modelling)
- reusable nappy (one for teacher modelling)
- pair of scissors (one for teacher modelling)
- photographs (or images projected on the visualizer) of two or three packages of different brands of nappies
- disposable nappy (one per group)
- reusable nappy (one per group)
- water
- A4 tray (two per group)
- pipette or syringe, measuring cylinders, weighing scales, paper towels (one set per group)
- various nappies to test. For example: different size nappies for different aged babies; different brands of disposable nappies; disposable nappies and eco-friendly disposable nappies (optional)
- A4 tray (five to six per group) (optional)

If using the Snap Science Year 5 Pupil Workbook you may not require the resource sheet below.

Snap Science Year 5 Pupil Workbook

- pages 34–35

Snap Science Year 5 Digital subscription

- Resource sheet 1: Record sheet – enlarged to A3 (one per child)

You will need (part 2)

- sticky-tack to display the information sheets
- highlighter pens (optional)

Snap resources:

- Resource sheet 1: Record sheet – to continue from part 1
- Resource sheet 2: Environmental impact information (A3 copies printed to display around the classroom) (Further copies for children to highlight in Part 2 as additional support)
- Resource sheet 3: Comparison table (one per child)
- Snapshot 1: Defining properties
- Snapshot 2: Why am I made from this?

Make sure you have opened/printed any *Snap* resources you intend to use in this lesson.

National Curriculum

Conceptual knowledge:

- compare and group together everyday materials on the basis of their properties, [including their hardness, [solubility], transparency, conductivity (electrical and thermal), and response to magnets]
- give reasons, based on evidence from comparative and fair tests, for the particular uses of everyday materials, including metals, wood and plastic

Working scientifically:

- taking measurements, using a range of scientific equipment, with increasing accuracy and precision, taking repeat readings when appropriate
- recording data and results of increasing complexity using scientific diagrams and labels, classification keys, tables, scatter graphs, bar and line graphs
- using test results to make predictions to set up further comparative and fair tests
- reporting and presenting findings from enquiries, including conclusions, causal relationships and explanations of and a degree of trust in results, in oral and written forms such as displays and other presentations

Scientific enquiry type:

- comparative testing

Key vocabulary	
Tier 2 vocabulary:	**Tier 3 vocabulary:**
design, dispose, leak, reuse	absorb/absorbent, compost, contamination, decompose, environment, impermeable, liquid, permeable

Health and safety Please refer to CLEAPSS for Health and Safety guidance and ensure that any identified hazards are managed appropriately.

Part 1: What is a nappy for? How can we compare reusable and disposable nappies?

Getting started

Throughout the lesson, model how to be mindful of wasting materials and sending too much waste to landfill. Remind children that they learned that objects which are not made from natural materials do not decompose (Year 4: Environmental Change). Keep the disassembly and use of nappies during the lesson to a minimum.

Ask: What is a nappy? What is it used for? Does anyone have a sibling who uses nappies at home? Share and discuss responses. Pass some disposable nappies around the class for children to have a closer look at. Ask: What makes a good nappy? What properties does a nappy need to have? Project a photograph (or a visualiser image) of the marketing information and claims from some of the packaging of different brands of nappies. Ask: What do the companies claim their nappies will do? Ask children to identify any information that might be useful, for example, does the packaging mention how much the nappy might absorb liquids without leaking? Record the responses on the board to create a 'good nappy criteria checklist'.

Show children the different parts of a disposable nappy by dissecting one with scissors. Demonstrate, using water and a tray, what each of the layers in the disposable nappy does:

a Water passes through the permeable top sheet. Ask: Why is it important that the liquid can pass through the material one way but not the other?

b A great deal of water is absorbed by the sodium polyacrylate powder and turns it into a gel. Ask: What do you think will happen when the gel is squeezed when full of water? Will there be a maximum amount of liquid the material can hold?

c Water doesn't pass through the impermeable backsheet. Ask: Why is this important? Explain that the outer layer is also waterproof to stop the nappy becoming dirty and getting wet from external sources.

Show children an example of a reusable nappy pointing out the various layers, components and fastening system. Ask: What material do you think this nappy is made from? There is no need to dissect this nappy as the parts should be clearly visible.

Explain that you have shown children two types of nappy: disposable and reusable. Ask: Why do you think there are two types? Discuss that nappies can either be thrown away or washed and reused. Tell them that there are many factors which parents consider when choosing a type of nappy: convenience, cost, comfort, efficiency and impact on the environment. Explain that it is important that parents are knowledgeable about the science involved to help make better decisions when answering the lesson question: **'Which is the best type of nappy?'**

Task

In groups of three to four, children then carry out a series of comparative tests to compare a disposable nappy and a reusable nappy.

Put children in groups of two to three to discuss how they will test for each property:

1. Ease of use: Ask: Is it easy to fasten and unfasten?
2. Comfort: Ask: Does it feel soft?
3. Flexible: Ask: Is the nappy easily bent, stretched and squashed?
4. Elastic: Ask: Does the nappy return to its original shape after it has been stretched or squashed?
5. Absorbent: Ask: What happens when water is added to the inner part of the nappy? How long does it take the liquid to be absorbed? How much liquid will it hold? If a lot of liquid has been absorbed what would it be like for the baby wearing it?
6. Leakproof: Ask: What happens if pressure is applied when the nappy is full of liquid? Does the water leak out? Would the elastic around the legs and waistband keep the water inside the nappy?
7. Waterproof: Ask: What happens when water is added to the back sheet of the nappy?

Ask: Which variables should we control in our comparative tests'? For example, ensuring the same amount of water is added to each type of nappy when testing if the nappy's back sheet is waterproof; applying the same pressure to each nappy full of liquid when testing to see if it is leakproof.

Each group should devise their own scale/system to rate each nappy against the property. For example: 1 being the hardest to use and 10 being the easiest to use; 1 being the least absorbent and 10 being the most absorbent. Discuss how the scale should work across all the tests so that an overall score can be given. Give each group a disposable nappy, a reusable nappy, water, two trays, a pipette or syringe, measuring cylinders, weighing scales and paper towels. Children carry out their tests and record their observations. They record their findings on Resource sheet 1: Record sheet.

Pupil Workbook: Complete Activity 1: Comparing reusable and disposable nappies on page 34.

Adaptations and support

An adult can support children by guiding them through the task, prompting and suggesting equipment to use where necessary. This group of children can record their findings and observations on a group record sheet.

Take it further

Children carry out a comparative test to explore how absorbent different nappies are. This test could focus on comparing: different size nappies for different aged babies; traditional disposable nappies and eco-friendly disposable nappies. Children need to decide on their enquiry question. Ask: What evidence do you need to collect from your practical investigation? They design their own record sheet, carry out their test and collect data. After the investigation is complete, give the children time to organise their results. Ask: What does your evidence show? Can you make a statement that summarises what you have learned about the nappies you have tested? How will you use your evidence to suggest to a parent which is the best nappy?

Reflect and review

Ask a few groups to share their test data. Ask: Which nappies fit our 'good nappy criteria checklist'? Did all of the groups have similar findings?

Discuss potential issues with the tests that have been carried out. Ask: Are the observations from the tests sufficient to make a decision about the effectiveness of the nappies? How might the tests be improved? When a baby is wearing the nappy what other things might need to be taken into account? Draw the children's attention to how they decided the amount of water to use in their tests. Ask: How might the amount of wee produced by the baby wearing the nappies change as they grow? Would the same amount of wee be produced every time?

Return to the advertising claims on the packaging. Ask: Which nappies do what the advertising claims the nappies can do? At this point in the lesson, ask children to consider the lesson question: **'Which is the best type of nappy?'**

Part 2: How do parents choose from the different types of nappies?

Getting started

Draw on children's knowledge of what happens to different materials when they are thrown away (Year 4: Environmental Change). Ask: What does environmentally friendly (or eco-friendly) mean? How can we care for planet Earth? Why is this important? Return to the advertising claims on the nappy packaging. Ask: Do any of the manufacturers mention environmental issues? Why do you think this might be?

Tell children that they are going to answer the following questions during the lesson: What are different types of nappy made from? How much do the different types of nappy cost? How much electricity does it take to wash and dry a reusable nappy? What might the impact be of using detergent to wash reusable nappies? How long do reusable nappies last? Do disposable nappies decompose? How much space in landfill do disposable nappies take up? Reassure children that it is difficult to make a decision about which nappy to choose as there are so many things to consider.

Task

Tell children they are going to learn about the environmental impact of using the different types of nappies using Resource sheet 2: Environmental impact information. Stick A3 copies of the resource sheets on display boards around the room. In pairs, children take turns to go and read one of the resource sheets then return to their partner to recount the information. This may take repeat visits. Together they make brief notes. They then swap roles and repeat the process with each information sheet.

Having read, and made notes, about all of the environmental information, ask children to pick out the main points about the types of nappy, deciding if they are negative or positive and record them on Resource sheet 3: Comparison table. They then use this information to help score the environmental impact of the nappy. Tell them to add an additional heading ('Eco-friendly score') in the empty column in their record sheet (Resource sheet 1 from Part 1). Discuss how they can give a rating in line with their other scores. Ask: What decision would you make about which nappy to use if you were a parent? What information has helped you to make this decision?

Explain that scientists are working on ways to develop eco-friendly disposable nappies that work in a similar way to a standard disposable nappy, but they are made from materials which are more environmentally friendly (plant-based materials). It is claimed that they decompose unlike traditional disposable nappies and the manufacturing process may use less electricity and/or chemicals. Some companies claim their nappies can be composted. They may be more expensive than disposable nappies as the cost of the materials used may be higher. Ask: Does this alter your decision about which nappy is best? Why? What do you think is the selling point of a biodegradable nappy?

Pupil Workbook: Complete Activity 2: Environmental impact of nappies on page 35.

Adaptations and support

Children can have printed copies of Resource sheet 2: Environmental impact information and pick out the key points with a highlighter pen. An adult can then discuss with children how/if these points have a negative or positive effect upon the environment.

Take it further

In pairs, children hold a debate. One child is presenting the case for using disposable nappies and the other is presenting the case for using reusable nappies. They plan out their arguments and counter arguments, then hold their mini debate.

Reflect and review

Having carried out their tests regarding the properties and heard about the environmental impact of using different types of nappy, ask: Why is it difficult to answer the question: **'Which is the best type of nappy?'** Explain that in science it isn't always simple to find an answer and that decisions in science can be complex. With nappies it is difficult to say which type of nappy meets all the requirements of a 'good' nappy and which is the most environmentally friendly. Allow a few children to take the hot seat as a 'nappy expert' to answer the question: What advice would you give to a new parent of a baby?

Answers

What criteria should be used to test the nappies?

Test to see if the nappy is: easy to use, comfortable, flexible, elastic, absorbent, leak-proof and waterproof.

Which nappy should I choose?

There is no one right answer when deciding which nappy to choose. Children base their decision on the evidence from the lesson. They should balance the evidence from their tests against the impact of using each nappy upon the environment, taking all arguments into account.

Homework suggestions

Complete some further research. Ask: Where at home are absorbent, permeable and waterproof materials used? In some countries sodium polyacrylate has been used when people's homes have been flooded. Ask: Is this helpful? What problems might be caused by using sodium polyacrylate in this way?

Assessment and evidence of learning

Children can:

- identify the properties of the different materials used in nappies including permeable, absorbent and waterproof materials
- utilise effective ways to test the different nappies for flexibility, elasticity, absorbency, water resistance and if the nappy is leakproof
- design and use a system or scale to rate the properties of each type of nappy
- summarise their results, making a general statement about what they found out
- use their scientific knowledge of materials and their properties in drawing conclusions
- pick out the key points when considering the environmental impact of the nappies: what they are made from; whether they decompose; the energy used; the water used; the potential contamination caused

- understand that other factors may influence parents' choice of nappy: cost and ease of use. They should appreciate that these factors may outweigh environmental considerations for some parents
- use their system or scale to rate the how environmentally friendly each type of nappy is
- use scientific vocabulary effectively to explain their understanding of the environmental impact of using different types of nappy
- appreciate that some scientific arguments are complex making it difficult to decide on the best solution.

If you are unsure that a child is able to identify the suitability of a variety of materials, then you can use Snapshots to check understanding and develop learning:

- Snapshot 1: Defining Properties
- Snapshot 2: Why am I made from this?

Module 3: Earth and space

Lesson 1: What's in space?

What children will learn and do

- Children learn about the main bodies found within and beyond our solar system.
- They learn that the Earth, Sun, Moon, planets and stars are all approximately spherical.
- They learn that the Sun is a star and the Earth is a planet.
- They learn about the relative sizes of the Earth, Sun, Moon and planets.
- They answer the lesson question: **'What's in space?'**

You will need

This lesson requires some pre-work. Before the start of this module, ask children to make observations of the night sky (in the evening or in the morning when it is still dark) and think about what they can see and how it changes.

- A2 sheets of paper, each with columns headed 'True', 'False' and 'Not sure' (one per group)
- a digital camera
- access to reference books or the internet to find information about our solar system (optional)

If using the Snap Science Year 5 Pupil Workbook you may not require all the resource sheets below.

Snap Science Year 5 Pupil Workbook

- pages 36–37

Snap Science Year 5 Digital subscription

- Resource sheet 1: Space card sort
- Slideshow 1: Journey into space
- Resource sheet 2: Planet data

Make sure you have opened/printed any *Snap* resources you intend to use in this lesson.

Save the cut-out cards from Resource sheet 1, as they will be needed for other lessons later in this module.

National Curriculum

Conceptual knowledge:

- describe the Sun, Earth and Moon as approximately spherical bodies

Working scientifically:

- recording data and results of increasing complexity using scientific diagrams and labels, [classification keys, tables, scatter graphs, bar and line graphs]

Scientific enquiry type:

- research using secondary sources of information

Key vocabulary	
Tier 2 vocabulary: diameter, spherical	**Tier 3 vocabulary:** diagram light, light source, moon, planet, solar system, star, Sun

Health and safety Please refer to CLEAPSS for Health and Safety guidance and ensure that any identified hazards are managed appropriately.

Getting started

Ask children if they made any observations of the night sky (pre-module task) and what they saw. Ask if they have ever been in places with lots of streetlights and places with no streetlights. Ask: What did the night sky look like? Was it different in different places? How does the sky look different in the daytime? Explain that, when there is less background light, the stars are easier to see; in a brightly lit area at night, only the brightest stars are visible. Explain that there are also stars in the daytime sky but they are not visible because of the brightness of the Sun, although sometimes we can still see the Moon. Remind children that it is dangerous to look directly at the Sun.

Tell children that today's lesson question is: **'What's in space?'** Explain that, as we cannot easily observe what is in space, children will be learning from observations made by scientists such as astronomers and astrophysicists. Tell them that the prefix 'astro' tells us that the word links to stars and space. Ask if they know any other words with this prefix (for example, astronaut). If they suggest 'astrology', explain that this is not considered to be a science although the word does show a link to the stars.

Ask children what they think is in space. If they suggest objects such as satellites or the space station, confirm that they are correct and tell them that the lesson focus is natural objects in space. Many of these can only be seen with a telescope, although sometimes the closest planets are visible to the naked eye. Introduce the term solar system to describe the Sun and the planets and other natural objects that go around it.

Split the class into groups of three or four. Give each group a set of cards cut out from Resource sheet 1: Space card sort, and an A2 sheet of paper with columns headed 'True', 'False' and 'Not sure'. Ask children to look at the cards, discuss the statements and decide which are true, which are false and which they are not sure about. This provides an indication of their current knowledge and ideas. Photograph them for later reference.

Discuss children's responses to statements 1–12, sharing knowledge from different groups and providing explanations to correct any misconceptions. Tell children that the other cards will be returned to in later lessons.

At the end of the discussion, children should know that:

- our Sun is one of many stars
- stars are light sources and also give off heat
- there are eight planets, including Earth, moving around our Sun
- the Earth has a moon, which we call the Moon
- some of the other planets also have moons
- the Earth, Sun and Moon are approximately spherical in shape, as are the other planets.

Display Slideshow 1: Journey into space. Show slide 1, which shows an illustration of the solar system, and confirm the names of the planets (Mercury, Venus, Earth, Mars, Jupiter, Saturn, Uranus, Neptune) and that they are the same shape but different sizes and different distances from the Sun (although not shown to scale). Note that the Moon is smaller than the planets and the Sun is only partially drawn as it is so huge.

Ask children to move any cards that they now think are in the wrong place, to demonstrate what they have learnt.

Pupil Workbook: Complete Activity 1: Space facts on page 36.

The task

Remind children of today's lesson question, 'What's in space?' Tell children that their task is to draw a labelled diagram showing what is in the solar system. To help them, they have some data collected by scientists. Display the planet data on slide 2 and ask questions to help children to interpret it. For example: Which planet is closest to the Sun? How do you know? Which is the largest planet? How do you know? What is its diameter? Which planet is similar in size to Earth?

Ask children to use what they have learnt so far, along with the planet data (which is also provided on Resource sheet 2), to draw a labelled diagram showing the Sun, planets and Moon. They could work on paper or in their exercise books.

Pupil Workbook: Complete Activity 2: The solar system on page 37.

Adaptations and support

Children who find it difficult to interpret data about size and position of the planets should concentrate on drawing them and labelling them in order of distance from the Sun (following the order of the planet names in the first column of the data table), without considering relative size. If needed, provide a print-out of Resource sheet 2 with the 'Diameter' column removed.

Take it further

Children could research how many moons each planet has and what other bodies can be found in the solar system (for example, asteroids), and add these to their diagram.

Reflect and review

Remind children of today's lesson question: **'What's in space?'**

Ask them to work with a partner, using their diagrams and other information they have learnt in the lesson, to agree an answer to the question. Take feedback from some pairs.

Answers

Getting started:

Cards 1–12:

1. We see stars in the sky because they reflect the Sun's light. FALSE (Stars are light sources; moons and planets are only visible because they reflect light from the Sun.)
2. Stars have a shape with points. FALSE (Stars are spherical, like planets and moons.)
3. Stars give off light from burning gases. TRUE
4. The Sun is a star. TRUE
5. There are a lot of stars in our solar system. FALSE (The only star in our solar system is the Sun. The other stars that we see are far beyond our solar system.)
6. The Sun and Moon are the same size. FALSE (They appear similar in size because the Sun is much further away. To demonstrate this effect, ask children to close one eye and move one finger so it appears the same size as you.)
7. There are many moons in the solar system. TRUE
8. The Sun, Moon and Earth are circular. FALSE (They are spherical; a circle is a 2D shape.)
9. The Sun is not a star because it doesn't shine at night. FALSE (Like the other stars, the Sun shines constantly but it is not always where we can see it.)
10. There are no other solar systems in space. FALSE (Scientists have discovered that many stars have their own planets and are the suns of their own solar systems.)
11. We see the Moon because it reflects the Sun's light. TRUE
12. There are eight planets in our solar system. TRUE

For reference in later lessons, where this content will be covered, the answers to cards 13–18 are:

13. The Moon goes round the Sun. FALSE (The Moon orbits the Earth – Lesson 5.)
14. The Earth goes round the Sun. TRUE (Lesson 2)
15. The Moon is a planet. FALSE (The Moon is a natural satellite of the Earth – Lesson 5.)
16. The Sun moves behind the Moon at night. FALSE (The Sun is not hidden behind anything at night; the part of the Earth that is in darkness is facing away from the Sun – Lesson 4.)
17. The Sun moves behind the Earth at night. FALSE (The Sun appears to move out of view behind the Earth at night, but this apparent movement is caused by the rotation of the Earth on its axis – Lesson 4.)

18. The Earth stays still and everything else moves around it. FALSE (The Earth orbits the Sun. The Sun, not the Earth, is at the centre of our solar system – Lesson 2.)

The task:

Children's diagrams should show the planets and the Moon as circles (to represent spheres) in order of distance from the Sun, similar to slide 1 but not in colour. Sizes and distances do not need to be to scale, but relative sizes should be roughly consistent with the data, for example, Earth and Venus shown as a similar size, with Mercury smaller and Jupiter much bigger.

Children's answers to the lesson question should include the correct names for the Sun, Moon and planets. They should also state that there are other moons (not named) within the solar system and more stars beyond it. Children may also include bodies such as asteroids, dwarf planets, planets around other stars, comets, meteors and meteorites, black holes, artificial satellites and the space station. These do not need defining or detailed discussion, but children could be encouraged to find out more outside the lesson.

Homework suggestions

Children could learn the mnemonic: My Very Educated Mother Just Served Us Noodles to remember the order of the planets. They could also teach it to someone else at home (or find out if they know a different one).

Encourage children to find out more about the other things found in space through reading, websites or television programmes.

Assessment and evidence of learning

Children can:

- represent the planets, Sun and Moon with circles, to show that they are spherical
- use data from a secondary source to present the relative sizes and positions of the Sun, Moon and planets.

Lesson 2: How do the planets move?

What children will learn and do

- Children learn about the orbital paths of the planets in our solar system.
- They model the orbital paths of the planets.
- They learn from secondary sources that the planets have different lengths of orbital paths and of year and identify a pattern in the data.
- They answer the lesson question: **'How do the planets move?'**

You will need

- a large indoor or outdoor space where you can draw on the ground with chalk
- eight balls, each labelled with the name of a planet; ideally these will be of different sizes to give an indication of the relative size of each planet (not to scale)
- string
- scissors
- chalk, ideally in eight different colours
- a tambourine or other instrument to beat time
- access to reference books or the internet to research 'heliocentric model' and 'geocentric model' (optional)

When preparing to teach the lesson, look back at where children placed cards 14 and 18 in the Lesson 1 card sort activity and use this to consider prior knowledge and direct your questioning.

If using the Snap Science Year 5 Pupil Workbook you may not require the resource sheet below.

Snap Science Year 5 Pupil Workbook

- pages 38–39

Snap Science Year 5 Digital subscription

- Animation 1: Planetary orbits
- Slideshow 1: How long is a year?
- Resource sheet 1: How do the planets move? (Prompts)

Make sure you have opened/printed any *Snap* resources you intend to use in this lesson.

National Curriculum

Conceptual knowledge:

- describe the movement of the Earth, and other planets, relative to the Sun in the solar system

Working scientifically:

- reporting and presenting findings from enquiries, including conclusions, [causal relationships and explanations of and degree of trust in results,] in [oral and] written forms [such as displays and other presentations]

Key vocabulary	
Tier 2 vocabulary: Spherical	**Tier 3 vocabulary:** data, diagram, model, observe orbit, pattern, planet, solar system, Sun, year

Health and safety Please refer to CLEAPSS for Health and Safety guidance and ensure that any identified hazards are managed appropriately.

Getting started

Ask children to look at their diagrams of the planets in the solar system from Lesson 1. Ask: How many planets are there? Are they still or moving? Where do they move? Children may remember from the last lesson, or already know, that the planets go around the Sun. Some may know the word orbit. If not, introduce it now.

Tell children that today's lesson question is: **'How do the planets move?'** They will only be considering the planets, not other bodies in or beyond the solar system.

Play Animation 1. Identify each of the planets and discuss how they move in their own separate orbits. Tell children that these orbits are almost circular.

Tell children that they are going to act out a model of how the planets move. Take the class into the playground or a large indoor space.

The task

Remind children of today's lesson question: **'How do the planets move?'**

Mark the Sun at the centre of the space. Tell children that they will start with the furthest planet from the Sun (Neptune). Ask a child to stand on the Sun and hold one end of a long length of string. Ask another child to represent Neptune; ask them to hold the other end of the string, go to the closest wall or boundary, and cut the string to that length. Tell them to tie the string to a piece of chalk and chalk a circle on the ground, keeping the string taut: the string acts like a pair of compasses.

Then repeat for the other planets. As a class, decide how far from the Sun each planet should be. Ask different children to represent each planet, cutting the string to an appropriate length and chalking their planet's orbit. If possible, use a different colour of chalk for each planet. Do not worry about relative distances of orbits from each other, just their order from the Sun.

Then choose eight different children to represent the planets; give each child a ball with a planet label. Ask why children think you have chosen balls to represent the planets and not, for example, bean bags or books, and confirm that this is because balls are spherical, like the planets. Ask each child to walk anticlockwise round the path of their orbit, holding their labelled ball.

When the planets have completed at least one orbit, pause to check that all children understand that the model shows the Sun at the centre of the solar system with all the planets moving around it (orbiting) in circular paths that do not overlap. Move the other planets away and ask the child representing the Earth to continue. Ask children how long it takes the Earth to make one complete orbit of the Sun, and confirm that it is one year.

Now choose another group of eight children to represent the planets, holding the labelled balls. Line them up along a radius of the circle and mark a starting point on each orbit. Ask what will happen if they all set off at the same time and move at the same speed. They should recognise that the inner planets will complete an orbit before the Earth, and the outer ones will complete an orbit after the Earth, because the paths are longer the further they are from the centre.

Demonstrate this by asking the 'planets' to walk (anticlockwise) around their paths in step, as you beat time with a tambourine. Ask the others to watch and check that the planet children stop when they get back to their markers. When the last child is back at the start, ask the class what they noticed.

Confirm that the term 'year' applies to the time it takes any planet to complete one orbit, and agree which planets have a shorter year than the Earth and which ones have a longer year.

Back in the classroom, prompt children to think more about an Earth year. Ask them how many days it has. Explain the following: Astronomers in the past, even though some of them thought the Sun orbited the Earth, were able to work out when a year had passed by observing how the position of the stars in the sky changed. They counted the number of days from the beginning to the end of the Earth's orbit and measured a year as 365 days. An orbit actually takes a little longer than 365 days – 365.25 days. After four years that adds up to one whole extra day. This is why we have the leap year when the 'extra' day is added onto February.

Display Slideshow 1, which shows data about the length of a year on each planet. Ask children to discuss with a partner whether this data fits with what they observed when modelling the orbits of the planets.

What pattern can they see in the data? Confirm that the further a planet is from the Sun the longer it takes to complete one orbit. Explain to the children that, not only do the outer planets have further to travel in each orbit but they also move more slowly so their years are much longer.

Ask children to provide a written answer, in their exercise books, to the lesson question: **'How do the planets move?'**

Pupil Workbook: Complete Activity 1: Movement of the planets on page 38 and Activity 2: How do planets orbit the Sun? on page 39.

Adaptations and support

Provide Resource sheet 1: How do the planets move?, which provides some prompts to help children to structure their answer to the lesson question: **'How do the planets move?'**

Take it further

Children could research and write the meanings of the terms 'heliocentric model' and 'geocentric model'. (This links to learning in Lesson 5.)

Reflect and review

Remind children of today's lesson question: **'How do the planets move?'**

Choose a child or two to share their answer to the lesson question, then discuss what makes a good answer.

Allow time for children to improve their answers.

Answers

Children's answers to the lesson question may include:

- The planets move in circular orbits around the Sun; these do not overlap.
- The Earth takes one year (365.25 days) to complete one orbit of the Sun.
- Planets closer to the Sun have shorter orbits and move more quickly, so the length of a year is shortest for the planets that are closest to the Sun.
- Planets further from the Sun have longer orbits and move more slowly, so the length of a year is greatest for the planets that are furthest from the Sun.
- For planets closer to the Sun than the Earth is, a year is shorter than an Earth year.
- For planets further from the Sun than the Earth is, a year is longer than an Earth year.

Homework suggestions

No suggested homework is assigned for this lesson.

Assessment and evidence of learning

Children can:

- correctly use the term 'orbit'
- describe the orbits of the planets as roughly circular paths that do not overlap
- state that the Earth takes one year to complete one orbit of the Sun
- use information from secondary sources to conclude that planets further from the Sun have longer orbital paths and so have longer years.

Lesson 3: How does the position of the Sun in the sky change?

What children will learn and do

- Children make observations of changing shadows over the course of a school day.
- They demonstrate practically, and observe using images, how the changing position of the Sun causes the changes to the shadows.
- They use diagrams to record and explain their observations.
- They answer the lesson question: **'How does the position of the Sun in the sky change?'**

You will need

This lesson will need to be completed across three days:

- Day 1: Teach the Getting started section the day before the observations are made.

- Day 2: Make the observations (first part of the Task) across the following whole school day.

- Day 3: Complete the lesson the following day, or as soon as possible afterwards.

The observations need to be made on a sunny day; you may need to teach this lesson out of sequence depending on the weather. Ideally, teach it earlier in the module, if poor weather is forecast.

- access throughout the school day to an area in the school grounds where it will be sunny all day, ideally where you can draw on the ground with chalk
- torches (one per group)
- pencils
- a 'shadow stick', e.g. a rounders post or other object that stands upright and will cast a straight shadow (you could also use a fixed feature such as a fence post, if suitably positioned)
- chalk (or string and tent pegs for use on grass)
- a digital camera
- sticky tack

If using the Snap Science Year 5 Pupil Workbook you may not require all the resource sheets below.

Snap Science Year 5 Pupil Workbook

- pages 40–41

Snap Science Year 5 Digital subscription

- Video 1: Changing shadows
- Slideshow 1: The path of the Sun
- Resource sheet 1: How does the position of the Sun in the sky change?
- Resource sheet 2: Making a shadow clock

Make sure you have opened/printed any *Snap* resources you intend to use in this lesson.

National Curriculum

Conceptual knowledge:

- use the idea of the Earth's rotation to explain day and night and the apparent movement of the Sun across the sky

Working scientifically:

- recording data and results of increasing complexity using scientific diagrams and labels, [classification keys, tables, scatter graphs, bar and line graphs]

Scientific enquiry type:

- observing change over time

Key vocabulary	
Tier 2 vocabulary: dawn, dusk, horizon, midday, sunrise, sunset	**Tier 3 vocabulary:** diagram, enquiry light, light source, opaque, pattern, predict/prediction, shadow, Sun

Health and safety Please refer to CLEAPSS for Health and Safety guidance and ensure that any identified hazards are managed appropriately.

Getting started

As noted above, the Getting started should be taught the day before children start the Task.

Ask children if they have noticed how the Sun sometimes shines directly in through the windows of the classroom (or the hall or a room at home, if your classroom is always in the shade). Ask: Does it shine into the room all day? Is the Sun always in the same place in the sky? What have you noticed about how its position changes? If children refer to the Sun being higher in the sky or visible for longer in summer, acknowledge this but tell them that the focus of this lesson is daily changes.

Play Video 1: **Changing shadows**. Remind the children that, in Year 3 (Module 2 Light and shadows), they **observed** how their own shadows (outdoors) and shadows they made in the classroom changed as the position of the light source changed.

Use a torch and a pencil held vertically on a table to demonstrate how an upright opaque object casts a shadow on the surface it is standing on. Ask children to predict what will happen when you move the torch higher and lower or to the left and right and relate this to how shadows changed in length and position in the video.

Tell children that the lesson question is: **'How does the position of the Sun in the sky change?'** They cannot observe and record the position of the Sun directly, because it is dangerous to look directly at it; this would damage their eyes. They will observe how a shadow changes during the day and use what they know about light to work out the changing position of the Sun.

The task

As noted above, the first part of the Task should be taught the day after the Getting started. Children will need to start making their observations first thing in the morning and continue throughout the day.

Remind children that the lesson question is: **'How does the position of the Sun in the sky change?'** Ask them what type of enquiry they think they will be using to gather evidence to answer the question (observing changes over different periods of time).

Set up a 'shadow stick' (an object that stands upright on the ground and will cast a straight shadow) in an area which is in sunlight all day and where it will not be disturbed. Ask a child to draw the shadow with chalk and label with the time. If the only available area is on grass, mark the length and position of the shadow using string and tent pegs.

Repeat observations at intervals throughout the day (aim for five to seven, ideally at equal intervals). Discuss how the shadow is changing in length and direction.

When all observations have been made, take a photograph to capture the complete set of observations.

The rest of the Task and the Reflect and review should be taught the following day.

In the classroom, display the photograph and ask children to discuss the patterns they can see. Confirm that the shadow decreases in length throughout the morning, is shortest around midday and increases again in the afternoon and that its position changes in an arc. Ask children to predict the length and position of the shadow an hour earlier in the morning and an hour later in the afternoon.

Provide each group with a torch, a pencil and a piece of adhesive tack. Ask them to use the adhesive tack to hold the pencil upright on their table. Give them some time to work out how to move their torch to recreate the pattern of shadows observed outside and shown in the photograph.

Choose a child from each group to trace the path of the Sun with their finger. Confirm that the path is a curve or arc across the sky, rising towards its highest point in the middle of the day. Encourage children to talk about the position of the Sun and the path, rather than describing it as moving across the sky.

Display Slideshow 1: The path of the Sun, showing slides 1–6 in sequence. For each slide, discuss what time of day it is showing, using words such as 'late morning' and 'evening', rather than times. Children should notice that in the first and last pictures the Sun is low, near the horizon. If children do not use them, introduce the terms sunrise, sunset, dawn and dusk. Draw attention to the compass, which shows that the observer is facing south. Tell children that the Sun rises in the east, is higher in the sky to the south at midday and sets in the west.

Remind children that the lesson question is: **'How does the position of the Sun in the sky change?'** Show slide 7 and explain that someone took photographs of the same place at different times on the same day, and then put the different positions of the Sun from all the photos onto one image to show how it changes position in the sky. Ask children to identify sunrise, sunset and midday and describe how the position of the Sun changes.

Next, show slides 8–17 in sequence. Each time the Sun changes position, ask children to predict the position of the tree's shadow and whether it will be longer or shorter. The shadow will then be revealed on the next slide.

Show slide 18, which shows a diagram of the changing position of the Sun and the changing shadows of the tree. Confirm that the changing position of the Sun creates the same pattern that children saw in their 'observing over time' enquiry the previous day.

Ask children to draw a labelled diagram to answer the lesson question: **'How does the position of the Sun in the sky change?'** Then ask them to draw a second diagram with annotations to explain how the changing position of the Sun explains their observations of the changing shadow of the 'shadow stick'.

Pupil Workbook: Complete Activity 1: Shadow enquiry on page 40 and Activity 2: The position of the Sun on page 41.

Adaptations and support

Provide children with Resource sheet 1 to support their recording.

Take it further

Children could discuss with a partner how the times of sunrise and sunset and the path of the Sun are different in summer compared to winter. If they are not sure, remind them that, in summer, the Sun rises earlier in the morning and sets later in the evening and is higher in the sky in the middle of the day. Ask them what difference this would make to the measurements of the shadows if they repeated their observations in the opposite season.

Reflect and review

Ask some of the children what they have learnt from their observation over time enquiry about how the position of the Sun in the sky changes and what difference this makes to shadows.

Show slide 19 of Slideshow 1 and ask if any of the children have seen a sundial. Do they know what it is for? Tell them that, before there were clocks, people used the position of the Sun in the sky to work out what time it was. A sundial or 'shadow clock' helps to make this method more accurate. Ask what time the sundial is showing (around 4 pm). How do they know? Tell them to talk to their partner about how a sundial works and take some responses. Discuss why the sundial only has numbers from 5 am to 8 pm (20:00) and what its limitations are for telling the time (not useful on cloudy days or at night).

Answers

The task:

Children's diagrams of the changing position of the Sun should be similar to the first diagram on Resource sheet 1. They should show some positions of the Sun and/or the path of the Sun and include labels for the time of day and the compass points (E, W and possibly S labelled on the diagram or a correctly orientated drawing of the main compass points).

Children's diagrams of the changing position of the shadow should be similar to the second one on Resource sheet 1, with shadow positions added (similar to the diagram on slide 18). Annotations will explain how the length and position of the shadow of the shadow stick changed during the school day because of the changing position of the Sun in the sky, with the shortest shadow when the Sun was highest in the sky and the shadow orientation changing from west to east as the sun moved from east to west.

If weather prevents this lesson being taught until after Lesson 4, children will be able to also include information about the rotation of the Earth causing the apparent movement of the Sun and the change in the shadows. This is not expected if the lessons are taught in sequence.

Take it further:

Children should describe the shadows as all being shorter for summer observations as the Sun is already higher in the sky at the start of the school day, rises even higher by midday than it does in winter and is still quite high at the end of the school day.

Homework suggestions

Children could use the instructions on Resource sheet 2 to make a shadow clock. They could then explain to someone at home how it works.

Assessment and evidence of learning

Children can:

- draw or describe the path of the Sun from east to west across the sky during a day
- use diagrams and annotations to present information about the changing position of the Sun in the sky and the effect of this on the length and position of shadows.

Lesson 4: What causes day and night?

What children will learn and do

- Children model the rotation of the Earth on its axis.
- They observe and explain how this causes day and night, the apparent movement of the Sun across the sky and the changes in shadow length and position they have previously observed.
- They answer the lesson question: **'What causes day and night?'**

You will need

- globes (one for demonstration, and one per group, if available)
- balls (one per group) if not enough globes are available
- torches (one per group) (a lamp is a useful alternative for the demonstration)
- small figures (one per group) or other small objects that will cast a clear shadow, e.g. matchsticks
- sticky tack
- the photograph from Lesson 3 of children's completed observations of the changing position of the shadow of the 'shadow stick'
- a device for recording voice or video (optional)

When preparing to teach the lesson, look back at where children placed cards 16 and 17 in the Lesson 1 card sort activity and use this to consider prior knowledge and direct your questioning.

If using the Snap Science Year 5 Pupil Workbook you may not require the resource sheet below.

Snap Science Year 5 Pupil Workbook

- page 42

Snap Science Year 5 Digital subscription

- Lesson 4 Animation 1: Planetary rotation
- Resource sheet 1: What causes day and night?
- Snapshot 1: Shadow sequence

Make sure you have opened/printed any *Snap* resources you intend to use in this lesson.

National Curriculum

Conceptual knowledge:

- use the idea of the Earth's rotation to explain day and night and the apparent movement of the Sun across the sky

Working scientifically:

- reporting and presenting [findings from enquiries, including conclusions, causal relationships and] explanations [of and degree of trust in results,] in oral and written forms [such as displays and other presentations]

Key vocabulary	
Tier 2 vocabulary:	**Tier 3 vocabulary:**
dawn, dusk, horizon, midday, sunrise, sunset	explain/explanation, model axis, dark/darkness, light, orbit, rotate, Sun

Health and safety Please refer to CLEAPSS for Health and Safety guidance and ensure that any identified hazards are managed appropriately.

Getting started

Ask children to show with their hands how the Earth moves in relation to the Sun. Ask: What is this movement called? (orbiting) How long does one orbit of the Earth around the Sun take? (365 days or one year.)

Tell children that they are going to watch an animation. Play Animation 1: Planetary rotation in full.

Choose two children to model what was shown in the animation. Child A represents the Sun. Give a globe to child B. Ask child B to hold the globe still and orbit the Sun, remembering to move anticlockwise. Remind children that this is how the Earth moves through space. Pause and ask child B to rotate or spin the globe on its axis in a clockwise direction as viewed from above. Ask how long it takes the Earth to complete one rotation and confirm that it is 24 hours or one day. Now ask child B to orbit the Sun while rotating the Earth on its axis to show how the Earth is rotating as it moves around the Sun. Ask how many rotations the Earth completes in one orbit of the Sun and confirm that it is 365, as each rotation is one day and there are 365 days in a year.

Tell children that today's lesson question is: **'What causes day and night?'** Explain that this is linked to the rotation of the Earth in the same way that the year is linked to the orbit of the Earth.

Reduce light levels in the classroom. Place the globe on a table and ask children to find their location on it. Mark the location with a small figure attached with sticky tack. Shine the lamp or torch onto the opposite side of the globe and ask children whether the figure can see the Sun. Confirm that they cannot; it is dark where they are so it is night. Slowly rotate the globe clockwise until the figure just moves into the light. Ask children what time of day it is now for the figure and confirm that it is dawn and they have just seen sunrise when the Sun appears over the horizon in the east. Move through the morning, pausing at midday when the Sun is highest in the sky, and the afternoon to dusk identifying when the figure will see sunset in the west. Continue through the night, pausing at midnight, to the next sunrise. Repeat the sequence as many times as is needed. Ask children what the figure will see the Sun doing in the sky and confirm that it will appear to change position and move across the sky. Ensure that children understand that the apparent movement of the Sun across the sky is caused by the rotation of the Earth; Although it is the Earth that is moving, the person on the Earth sees the changing position of the Sun in the sky.

Pupil Workbook: Complete Activity 1: Earth's orbit and rotation on page 42.

The task

Provide each group with a globe or ball, a torch, a figure and sticky tack. Ask them to use these to model the rotation of the Earth as you did, paying attention to the shadow of the figure as it moves through daytime. Show the photograph of the shadow observations from Lesson 3 and confirm that the shadow of the figure on the globe/ball changes in a similar way. The changing shadows are caused by the rotation of the Earth, which creates the apparent movement of the Sun across the sky.

Tell children that they are going to create a commentary, as in the animation they saw earlier, to accompany their modelling of the rotation of the Earth and explain what causes day and night. Display, or provide for each group, Resource sheet 1: What causes day and night?, which shows a list of vocabulary to include.

Ask children to create and rehearse their commentary orally as a group. When each group is ready, they could record their commentary.

Then ask children, working individually, to answer the lesson question: **'What causes day and night?'** by writing a commentary in their exercise books.

Pupil Workbook: Complete Activity 2: Day and night on page 42.

Adaptations and support

Include images or symbols on the vocabulary list as additional support.

As an alternative to writing the commentary, children could sequence key words as a reminder and present their commentary orally, using the model if necessary. This could be recorded as sound or video.

Take it further

Children could extend the commentary to include elements of the model from the start of the lesson (with child A and child B), along with the earth orbiting the Sun as it rotates on its axis.

Reflect and review

Choose a country in a different time zone, perhaps where someone in the class has friends or family. Mark it on the globe. Choose a child to read their commentary aloud and use the torch and globe to demonstrate that the explanation for **'What causes day and night?'** is still true for a country elsewhere on the globe. As a class, discuss how clear the commentary was and whether improvements are needed.

Ask children with friends and family in other countries if they have ever noticed, when speaking to them by phone or video call, whether it is a different time of day in the other country. Attach one figure to the UK on the globe using sticky tack and attach another figure on a country in a different time zone. Demonstrate that, although both countries follow the pattern of day and night, sunrise, midday and sunset happen at different times for each country. Compare approximately what time of day or night it is in the other country when it is sunrise, sunset or midday in the UK.

Answers

The task:

Children's commentaries should use the vocabulary provided to describe the sequence of sunrise, morning, midday, afternoon, sunset, night, referring to the position of the Sun at different times of day and its apparent movement across the sky and identifying the cause as the rotation of the Earth on its axis. They should include the information that a day is 24 hours, which is the time for one complete rotation. They may also refer to how the shadows change (not essential information to answer the question).

Take it further:

Children should also include the information that the Earth, while rotating on its axis, is orbiting the Sun. It takes one year to orbit the Sun, during which the Earth rotates 365 times (or 365 and a quarter times) on its axis.

Homework suggestions

Children could choose a country either where they know someone, that they have visited or that they would like to visit. They can then use an atlas or website to find out where it is, and what time it is there at the time the child is doing their homework. They could work out when would be a good time to call someone who lives there (a time when neither person will be asleep).

Assessment and evidence of learning

Children can:

- demonstrate and describe the rotation of the Earth on its axis
- use this to explain what causes day and night and the apparent movement of the Sun across the sky
- present their explanation as a written or oral commentary to accompany a simple model.

If you are unsure if a child can use the idea of the Earth's rotation to explain day and night and the apparent movement of the Sun across the sky, you can use the Snapshot 1: Shadow sequence to check understanding and develop the learning.

Lesson 5: How does the Moon move?

What children will learn and do

- Children model how the Moon orbits and rotates.
- They identify evidence that supports the model.
- They recreate historical models of the universe to explore how and why ideas changed and compare them with current knowledge.
- They answer the lesson question: **'How does the Moon move?'**

You will need

Before the start of this module, children will have made observations of the night sky and considered what they can see and how it changes. In Lesson 1, this pre-module work was drawn upon, with a focus on what children could see. In this lesson, children will need to think back about any changes they noticed in the shape of the Moon.

- a large indoor or outdoor space
- a torch
- a pale-coloured ball (approximately football-sized)
- thick paper or card labels: one each of 'Sun', 'Moon', 'Earth', the other planets and four or five saying 'stars'

When preparing to teach the lesson, look back at where children placed cards 13 and 15 in the Lesson 1 card sort activity and use this to consider prior knowledge and direct your questioning.

If using the Snap Science Year 5 Pupil Workbook you may not require all the resource sheets below.

Snap Science Year 5 Pupil Workbook

- pages 43–45

Snap Science Year 5 Digital subscription

- Resource sheet 1: Modelling changing ideas about the solar system (teacher instructions)
- Resource sheet 2: Scientist scripts
- Resource sheet 3: How does the Moon move? (optional)
- Resource sheet 4: Models of the solar system (optional)

Make sure you have opened/printed any *Snap* resources you intend to use in this lesson.

National Curriculum

Conceptual knowledge:

- describe the movement of the Earth, and other planets, relative to the Sun in the solar system
- describe the movement of the Moon relative to the Earth

Working scientifically:

- identifying scientific evidence that has been used to support or refute ideas or arguments

Key vocabulary	
Tier 2 vocabulary:	**Tier 3 vocabulary:**
Spherical	diagram, evidence, explain/explanation, model axis, moon, orbit, planet, rotate, solar system, star, support, Sun

Health and safety Please refer to CLEAPSS for Health and Safety guidance and ensure that any identified risks are managed appropriately.

Getting started

Use questioning and paired discussion to recap key learning so far about the solar system:

- The Sun is the star at the centre of our solar system.
- There are eight spherical planets which orbit the Sun; one complete orbit is a year.
- Each planet also rotates on its axis, causing day and night.
- There are other bodies such as moons and dwarf planets in our solar system.

Tell children that, now they have learned about how the planets move, today's lesson question is: **'How does the Moon move?'** Ask them what they already know about this and confirm that the Moon orbits the Earth. Explain that, although it is spherical and looks like a small planet, it is not a planet because it does not orbit the Sun. Some children may also know, or guess, that the Moon rotates on its axis.

Choose children to model how the Moon moves in relation to the Earth. One child represents the Earth and the other child holds a pale-coloured ball to represent the Moon. Tell the child holding the ball to orbit the Earth. The child representing the Earth can stand still, but remind children that the Earth is actually orbiting the Sun and rotating on its axis.

Remind children that they have looked at how the movements of the Earth link to the measurements of a day and year and ask if they can work out what measurement of time links to the movement of the Moon. Explain that one orbit of the Moon takes 28 days, which is a lunar month. It is not quite the same as a calendar month, because these have had days added to them so they fit exactly into the 365 days of a year.

Standing on the opposite side of the Earth to the Moon, shine the torch onto the ball, reminding children that we can only see the Moon because it is illuminated by the Sun. The child representing the Earth should see a full moon. Ask the child representing the Moon to start orbiting again. As the Moon completes an orbit, draw attention to the fact that the illuminated side of the Moon does not always face the Earth. Although children do not need to know the detail of this, it is why the Moon changes in appearance during the month and is scientific evidence for the Moon orbiting the Earth.

Ask children to think back to the pre-module task, when they looked at the night sky. Ask whether anyone **observed** the different shapes or phases of the Moon. What shapes did they see?

Remove the torch. Make a pen mark on the ball and tell the child holding it to rotate as they orbit the Earth so that the mark is always facing the Earth. Tell children that the Moon rotates slowly on its axis, taking 28 days to complete one rotation so the same side of the Moon always faces the Earth. The scientific evidence for this is that we can always see the same craters and mountains, which make the 'face' known as the man in the moon.

Pupil Workbook: Complete Activity 1: Moon phases on page 43.

The task

Remind children that our current knowledge about our solar system and the rest of the universe comes from **observations** made by scientists on Earth, astronauts and equipment in space (space station, probes, telescopes, and so on). Tell them that in the past scientists did not have the powerful equipment that we have now, so their observations were limited and they created different **models** of the solar system and universe to explain what they could see. Ideas have changed as scientists made new observations and needed new models to explain them.

Take children into a large indoor or outdoor space. Use the teacher instructions on Resource sheet 1: Modelling changing ideas about the solar system and give children the scripts that are provided on Resource sheet 2: Scientist scripts. Ask children to model and dramatise how and why ideas about the solar system and universe have changed. Children who completed the Take it further task in Lesson 2 could be asked to identify geocentric and heliocentric models.

After creating the different models, pause the other movements, focus attention onto the Earth and Moon and remind children that today's lesson question is: **'How does the Moon move?'** Ask children to describe how the Moon moves. Ask them what evidence supports this description of the way the Moon moves. Confirm that it is the observations that: (1) the same craters and other features on the Moon are always visible from Earth; and (2) the Moon as seen from Earth appears to change shape. If children also suggest the apparent movement of the Moon across the sky, explain that, like the apparent movement of the Sun across the sky, this is caused by the rotation of the Earth.

Ask children to use words or an annotated diagram to answer the question: **'How does the Moon move?'** They should work in their exercise books. They should also answer the question: What scientific evidence supports your answer?

Pupil Workbook: Complete Activity 2: Models of the solar system on page 44 and Activity 3: How the Moon moves on page 45.

Adaptations and support

Children who need support with recording can use Resource sheet 3: How does the Moon move?

Take it further

Working with a partner, children could use the diagrams from Resource sheet 4: Models of the solar system and a copy of the scripts (Resource sheet 2) to create a timeline of different models of the solar system. For each model, they could include a piece of evidence that supported it.

Reflect and review

Remind children of the lesson question: **'How does the Moon move?'** and that they should also have answered the question, 'What scientific evidence supports your answer?' Choose a child to share their work. Discuss how clearly they have answered the questions, using diagrams and/or a written explanation. Allow time for children to improve their answers.

Remind them that scientific ideas change when there is new evidence. As modern scientists are using more powerful telescopes and space probes to explore beyond our solar system, new ideas about the universe are still being developed.

If any children have completed the Take it further task, ask them to share their timelines.

Answers

The task:

Children's answers to the lesson question should describe, or show in an annotated diagram, the Moon orbiting the Earth once every 28 days and rotating on its axis once every 28 days. They may also indicate that, while this is happening, the Earth is also orbiting the Sun and rotating on its axis.

As scientific evidence for their answers, children should identify the changing shape of the Moon in the sky and observations that the same features of the Moon are always visible from Earth.

Take it further:

Children should produce something similar to this:

- 300 BCE [Ancient Greek astronomer's model] Evidence: It is not possible to feel the Earth moving, but the Sun and Moon move across the sky.
- 200 CE [Ptolemy's model] Evidence: There are five planets that wander across the sky in a different way to the stars.
- 1600s [Galileo's model] Evidence: More observations of the movements of the planet have been made which cannot be explained by a geocentric model. Or: Observations through a telescope of Moon craters and the moons of Jupiter.
- 1845 [Galle's model] Observations of Uranus and Neptune made by more powerful telescopes.

Homework suggestions

Children could find out about recent advances in space exploration and observation, for example the Hubble Telescope and James Webb Space Telescope (JWST), the Perseverance Mission to Mars, the International Space Station, Voyager 2.

Assessment and evidence of learning

Children can:

- describe in writing and/or diagrams how the Moon orbits the Earth and rotates on its axis
- create a model of the solar system with all the planets orbiting in the correct order from the Sun, and the Moon orbiting the Earth
- recognise observations of the Moon that provide evidence for how it moves.

Lesson 6: What patterns can we find in data about the planets?

What children will learn and do

- Children learn how to interpret a scatter graph.
- They identify patterns from scatter graphs.
- They revisit and consolidate conceptual knowledge from across the module.
- They answer the lesson question: **'What patterns can we find in data about the planets?'**

You will need

- A2 sheets of paper, each with columns headed 'True', 'False' and 'Not sure' (one per group)
- photographs of the original group card sorts from Lesson 1
- highlighter pens (one per group)
- access to reference books or the internet to research data about the planets (optional)
- spreadsheet software (optional)

If using the Snap Science Year 5 Pupil Workbook you may not require all the resource sheets below.

Snap Science Year 5 Pupil Workbook

- pages 46–49

Snap Science Year 5 Digital subscription

- Slideshow 1: Interpreting scatter graphs
- Resource sheet 1: What patterns can we find in data about the planets?
- Resource sheet 2: Data about the planets (optional)
- Lesson 1 Resource sheet 1: Space card sort
- Snapshot 1: Solar system
- Snapshot 2: The Moon

Make sure you have opened/printed any *Snap* resources you intend to use in this lesson.

You should not need to print new copies of Lesson 1 Resource sheet 1 if you have saved the cut-out cards from Lesson 1.

National Curriculum

Conceptual knowledge:

- describe the movement of the Earth, and other planets, relative to the Sun in the solar system
- describe the movement of the Moon relative to the Earth
- describe the Sun, Earth and Moon as approximately spherical bodies
- use the idea of the Earth's rotation to explain day and night and the apparent movement of the Sun across the sky

Working scientifically:

- recording data and results of increasing complexity using [scientific diagrams and labels, classification keys, tables,] scatter graphs, [bar and line graphs]

Scientific enquiry type:

- pattern seeking

Key vocabulary	
Tier 2 vocabulary:	**Tier 3 vocabulary:**
Diameter	data, model, predict/prediction
	moon, orbit, pattern, planet, solar system, Sun

Health and safety Please refer to CLEAPSS for Health and Safety guidance and ensure that any identified hazards are managed appropriately.

Getting started

Ask children to think back to Lesson 2 when they learned how the planets in the solar system move around the Sun. Ask them to recall, with a partner:

- the names of the planets in their order from the Sun (Mercury, Venus, Earth, Mars, Jupiter, Saturn, Uranus, Neptune)
- the word for the movement of a planet around a sun (and a moon around a planet) (orbit)
- what pattern they found for the length of a year on different planets (the further a planet is from the Sun, the longer it takes to complete one orbit, which is a year on that planet).

Tell children that today's lesson question is: **'What patterns can we find in data about the planets?'** Remind them that they identified the pattern for distance from the Sun and year length for a planet by modelling the movements and comparing what they found with a table of secondary data collected by scientists. Explain that this works well for a small amount of data, but when scientists are looking for patterns in a large amount of data, they find it easier to see patterns if they use a scatter graph.

Display Slideshow 1: Interpreting scatter graphs. Explain how slide 1 shows the data from the table used in Lesson 2. Then show slide 2, which represents the data in a scatter graph. Identify which point represents the data for each planet. Explain the following: In a scatter graph, the two variables are plotted against each other as points which are not joined up with a line. The points show a pattern of length of year increasing and the distance from the Sun increasing, so the points are arranged upwards from bottom left to top right of the graph. Ideally, scientists would need more than eight data points in their sample to be sure that they have found a pattern, but there are only eight planets in the solar system.

Show slide 3. Ask children to think about distance from the Sun and surface temperature. What pattern do they predict this data will show? Show slide 4 and discuss how the graph shows that planets that are further from the Sun are usually colder; the points are arranged from top left to bottom right of the graph. One planet does not fit the pattern; ask children to use the table to work out which planet this is. Explain that Venus is unusual because it heats up very easily.

Remind children that the other data they were given earlier in the module was the diameter of each planet. Show the table on slide 5 and ask children they can identify a pattern. Then show the graph on slide 6 and confirm that there is no pattern; the data points are randomly arranged and there is no link between size of planet and distance from the Sun. Tell children that it is important to be able to recognise when there is no pattern.

Pupil Workbook: Complete Activity 1: Do planets further from the Sun have longer years? on page 46.

The task

Remind children that today's lesson question is: **'What patterns can we find in data about the planets?'**

Tell them that you are going to give them some enquiry questions about the planets and scatter graphs of data collected to answer them. They will use the graphs to decide whether there is a pattern and, if there is one, to state what it is.

Provide children with Resource sheet 1: What patterns can we find in data about the planets? For each pattern seeking enquiry question and graph on the sheet, children identify whether there is a pattern in the data and use this to answer the question.

Pupil Workbook: Complete Activity 2: Do larger planets have more moons? on page 47, Activity 3: Do larger planets have longer years? on page 48 and Activity 4: Do planets that are further from the Sun move more quickly? on page 49.

Adaptations and support

Some children may need a printout of Slideshow 1 as a reminder of the patterns.

Take it further

Children could identify their own question to answer, from the data set on Resource sheet 2: Data about the planets or from their own research. They could use spreadsheet software to plot a scatter graph and identify the pattern.

Reflect and review

Review children's answers to the enquiry questions and discuss any misunderstandings. Remind children that they were looking for patterns in data for two variables where they could not influence them or control other variables.

Put children in the same groups as they were in for the card sort activity in Lesson 1. Provide each group with the space cards (Lesson 1 Resource sheet 1) and a sheet of A2 paper with headings 'True', 'False' and 'Not sure'. Ask children to sort the cards to show what they now know at the end of the module. For any statements that are false, children should write next to it a true version of the statement.

If any groups still have cards in the 'Not sure' column, give them the opportunity to look in their books or send one child from their group to find out by looking at other groups' responses. Check responses and address any remaining misconceptions.

Give each group the photograph of their original card sort and a highlighter pen. Ask them to highlight all the ones that show they now know something they did not know at the start of the module.

Answers

The task:

Children's answers to the enquiry questions on Resource sheet 1 should identify the following patterns:

1. Do larger planets have more moons? Yes, the pattern is that larger planets have more moons, although not all planets fit the pattern exactly.
2. Do larger planets have longer years? There is no pattern linking size of planet and length of year.
3. Do planets that are further from the Sun move more quickly? No, the pattern is that the planets that are further from the Sun move more slowly than the closer ones.

Reflect and review:

For answers to the card sort activity, see the lesson plan for Lesson 1.

Homework suggestions

Children could explain to someone at home their three favourite new things that they have learned during this module.

Assessment and evidence of learning

Children can:

- interpret a scatter graph, identifying and stating a pattern and recognising when there is no pattern
- correctly identify true and false statements about all conceptual knowledge taught in the module and correct the false ones.

If you are unsure if a child can describe the movement of the Earth, and other planets, relative to the Sun in the solar system, you can use the Snapshot 1: Solar system to check understanding and develop the learning.

If you are unsure if a child can describe the movement of the Moon relative to the Earth, you can use the Snapshot 2: The Moon to check understanding and develop the learning.

Module 4: Plant and animal life cycles

Lesson 1: How do flowering plants produce seeds?

What children will learn and do

- Children learn about the life cycle of flowering plants.
- They revisit learning about pollination and seed formation.
- They dissect a flower and identify and draw the reproductive organs.
- They create a resource to explain to someone else the process of how flowering plants reproduce.
- They answer the lesson question: **'How do flowering plants produce seeds?'**

You will need

- flowers for dissection such as alstroemeria/tulips/daffodils (one per pair)
- strips of paper (one per pair)
- magnifiers (one per pair)
- modelling clay (optional)
- audio recorders (optional)
- video recorders (optional)
- access to reference books or the internet to research wind-pollinated and animal-pollinated plants (optional)

If using the Snap Science Year 5 Pupil Workbook you may not require all the resource sheets below.

Snap Science Year 5 Pupil Workbook

- pages 50–52

Snap Science Year 5 Digital subscription

- Resource sheet 1: Flower power
- Animation 1: Parts of the flower
- Resource sheet 2: Life cycle
- Resource sheet 3: Flower structure (optional)
- Resource sheet 4: Flower dissection checklist
- Resource sheet 5: True/False/Not always cards

Make sure you have opened/printed any *Snap* resources you intend to use in this lesson.

National Curriculum

Conceptual knowledge:

- describe the life process of reproduction in some plants and animals

Working scientifically:

- recording data and results of increasing complexity using scientific diagrams and labels, [classification keys, tables, scatter graphs, bar and line graphs]

Key vocabulary	
Tier 2 vocabulary: dissect	**Tier 3 vocabulary:** anther, carpel, female, fertilisation, filament, flower, male, ovary, ovule, pollen, pollination, pollinator, reproduction, stamen, stigma, style

Health and safety Please refer to CLEAPSS for Health and Safety guidance and ensure that any identified risks are managed appropriately.

Green Plant Code

- Always wash your hands after handling plants.
- Remember that some plants can be poisonous or cause allergic reactions in some people. Use gardening gloves if handling plants.
- Do not eat plants you find outside.
- Do not pick wild plants.

Getting started

Tell children that, in this module, they will be learning about all sorts of life cycles. Ask them to recall what they learnt about the life cycle of flowering plants in Year 3 (Module 6, Flowering plants life cycle). Explain that for the first three lessons of the module they will be looking at plants, and in later lessons they will explore the life cycles of some animals.

Have a look at the three flowers in Resource sheet 1: Flower power. Ask children: What can you see? What is the same or different about these flowers? Do they know the names of any of the parts of the flower?

Children can see the insides of three flowers – alstroemeria, tulip and daffodil. They can see the reproductive parts of each of these flowers. They all have male and female reproductive parts.

Explain the following: The alstroemeria has stripes on it to guide a pollinator into the flower. This helps it to be pollinated by insects. In the yellow daffodil, the anthers are covered with fluffy pollen. The reproductive organs within the flowers are slightly different shapes. Tell children that today they are going to investigate the lesson question: **'How do flowering plants produce seeds?'**

The task

Show children Animation 1: Parts of the flower. Check their understanding of the processes of pollination and fertilisation that are shown. Ask: Where is pollen produced? How is it transferred onto the female part of the plant (the carpel)? What happens then?

Give children Resource sheet 2: Life cycle. Ask them to sequence the flower life cycle cards.

In pairs, the children then dissect a flower so that they can see first-hand the structures involved in forming a seed. They may wish to use Resource sheet 3: Flower structure to help them identify the structures on their flower. As they work, encourage the children to use a magnifier to help them to look in detail at the flower structures and make detailed drawings of what they see. Resource sheet 4: Flower dissection checklist gives the steps of the flower dissection process (copied below). Teachers may like to model how to do a flower dissection first.

1. Examine your intact flower. Draw a sketch of it. What shape is it?
2. How would an insect get into it to gather nectar? Are there any markings on the petals which would encourage a pollinator in? If a flower is brightly coloured, has a scent or is open shaped, this is probably to advertise its presence to animal pollinators such as insects, bats and birds.
3. Does the flower have any sepals? These protected the petals when they were developing. Add labels to your drawing.
4. Carefully remove the petals from the flower. Lay them out on the strip of paper. How many are there? Do they have any markings on them?
5. How many stamens are there? Pick them off carefully. Look at one closely and draw it on your sheet. Label the anther and filament. Brush one carefully with your finger. Does any pollen stick to your finger?
6. This leaves the carpel, which houses the female reproductive parts of the flower. Have a good look at and draw a picture of it. At the top is the stigma. What shape is it? This is the place where the pollen grain would stick if the flower was pollinated. Then there is the style, which leads to the ovary where the ovules are stored.

7. It is possible to split the ovary in half with a fingernail. Inside are the ovules, which can be observed either by eye or more closely with a magnifier. If the eggs in the ovules were fertilised, they would develop into seeds.

Return to the lesson question: **'How do flowering plants produce seeds?'** Ask children to use their drawings to describe to each other the process of how flowers produce seeds. Then ask them to work in pairs to create an 'explainer' so they can teach this to other learners. For example: a storyboard/cartoon strip, voiceover or a modelling clay model with accompanying video commentary, explaining the process.

Pupil Workbook: Complete Activity 1: Life cycle of a flower on page 50, Activity 2: Flower dissection on page 51 and Activity 3: Flower parts on page 52.

Adaptations and support

Some children will need support with fine motor control, when pulling apart their flowers. Children can use Resource sheet 3: Flower structure to help them to notice the parts of a flower.

Take it further

Remind children that not all plants are pollinated by animals. Some flowers are pollinated by wind. Ask children to find some images of wind- pollinated plants. What do they notice?

Ask children to make a list of wind-pollinated or animal-pollinated plants. This can be done on a nature walk outside or as a research activity.

Reflect and review

Ask children to share their 'explainers' with one another and give each other helpful feedback. Ensure that there is time for the children to utilise this feedback to develop their work. Return to the lesson question: How do flowering plants produce seeds? Ask: Do the explainers answer it? What science have they done to gather the evidence to answer the question?

Ask children to look back at their flowering plant life cycles card they sequenced. Ask: What would happen if there were no bees or insects to pollinate the plants? How would this affect their life cycle?

Check what children can remember about reproduction in flowering plants using Resource sheet 5: True/False/Not always cards. Children work in groups to sort the statements into true, false and not always true.

Pupil Workbook: Complete Activity 4: True or false? on page 52.

Answers

What is pollination? Pollen is a small, powdery substance found on the anther part of the stamen. Flowers need pollen from another plant of the same type to be pollinated. Pollen can be moved from plant to plant either by the wind or by pollinating animals such as bees and butterflies.

What is fertilisation in plants? Inside a grain of pollen is the male sex cell which fertilises with the ovule, the female sex cell, from which a seed is formed.

Take it further

Wind-pollinated plants don't normally have flowers, but when they do they are small, don't have perfumes or nectar, produce large amounts of light pollen, have stamens and s carpels exposed to air currents to either catch or distribute pollen, and don't normally have flower petals. Wind-pollinated plants produce larger quantities of light, dry pollen from small, plain flowers that can be carried on the wind.

TRUE/FALSE/NOT ALWAYS CARDS

1. The carpel is the female part of the flower, where the seed is made. **TRUE** – The carpel is the female reproductive organ of a flower, consisting of an ovary, a stigma, and usually a style. It may occur singly or as one of a group.
2. The stamens are the male part of the flower. They produce pollen. **TRUE**
3. Flowers are only pollinated by insects. **NOT ALWAYS** – Flowers can be pollinated by wind, water, insects and other animals, such as bats and birds.
4. Some plants don't have colourful flowers. **TRUE**
5. Seeds are always found inside fruit. **NOT ALWAYS** – Some plants such as strawberries have seeds on the outside of the fruit.
6. Only some flowers produce nectar. **TRUE** – Not all flowers produce nectar. Wind-pollinated flowers do not need to attract pollinators so do not produce nectar.

Homework suggestions

Children can choose from one of these activities:

1. Have a look for seeds where you live. Collect and draw some of the seeds you find.
2. Design and make a seed. How will it spread? Will it be dispersed on the wind, or in water, or by animal?
3. Make your own flower. Make sure your flower has sepals, petals, stamens , pollen and a carpel).

Assessment and evidence of learning

Children can:

- describe the life process of sexual reproduction in flowering plants, including pollination and fertilisation
- explain the role of different parts of the flower in sexual reproduction
- make accurate labelled drawings of the parts of the flower.

Lesson 2: Do all plants have the same number of reproductive parts?

What children will learn and do

- Children compare two different flowers.
- They go on a nature walk outside and compare more flowers.
- They learn that different flowers have different numbers of petals, stamens or carpels, and that this helps botanists to identify them.
- They answer the lesson question: **'Do all plants have the same number of reproductive parts?'**

You will need

- flowers to dissect (two different types per group of four)
- clipboards and pencils
- magnifiers
- camera (optional)
- access to reference books or the internet to research botanists (optional)

If using the Snap Science Year 5 Pupil Workbook you may not require all the resource sheets below.

Snap Science Year 5 Pupil Workbook

- pages 53–55

Snap Science Year 5 Digital subscription

- Resource sheet 1: Flower vocabulary
- Resource sheet 2: Flower comparison
- Resource sheet 3: Flower tally chart

Make sure you have opened/printed any *Snap* resources you intend to use in this lesson.

National Curriculum

Conceptual knowledge:

- describe the life process of reproduction in some plants and animals

Working scientifically:

- recording data and results of increasing complexity using [scientific diagrams and labels, classification keys], tables, [scatter graphs, bar and line graphs]
- reporting and presenting findings from enquiries, including conclusions, causal relationships and explanations of and degree of trust in results, in oral [and written] forms [such as displays and other presentations]

Scientific enquiry type:

- pattern seeking

Key vocabulary	
Tier 2 vocabulary: Dissect	**Tier 3 vocabulary:** anther, carpel, filament, flower, ovary, ovule, pollen, seed, stamen, stigma

Health and safety Please refer to CLEAPSS for Health and Safety guidance and ensure that any identified hazards are managed appropriately.

Green Plant Code

- Always wash your hands after handling plants.

- Remember that some plants can be poisonous or cause allergic reactions in some people. Use gardening gloves if handling plants.
- Do not eat plants you find outside.
- Do not pick wild plants.

Getting started

Remind children that in this module they are learning about life cycles, and that they are starting off by focusing on plants. Revisit the learning from Lesson 1 about the reproductive parts of flowering plants and how seeds are produced

Ask children to work in groups. Give each group the cards cut out from Resource sheet 1: Flower vocabulary. Ask them to match the name of each flower part with a label describing its function.

Tell children that today they are going to investigate the lesson question: **'Do all plants have the same number of reproductive parts?'**

Pupil Workbook: Complete Activity 1: Parts of a flower on page 53.

The task

Tell children that to find out the answer to the question they are going to compare different flowers.

In groups of four, ask children to work in pairs. Each pair will dissect a different flower.. Using the same method as in Lesson 1, they will slowly and carefully take the flower apart and record their observations on Resource sheet 2: Flower comparison. Support children to look carefully at each flower and then compare them with each other. Show them how to use a magnifier to help them to look really closely at each flower's reproductive structures.

Ask: Did the flowers have the same number of stamens? How were the two flowers different?

Next, take the children outside to look at flowers in your school grounds. Ask: How are they similar or different? Ask children to work in pairs. Provide each pair with a magnifier and Resource sheet 3: Flower tally chart. Ask them to find as many different types of flower as possible and record colour and number of stamens in the tally chart.

NB: Daisy-like flowers are composite flowers with many, many small florets making up one flower. Examples include aster, daisy, ragweed, thistle or sunflowers. So on the flower tally chart children would tick more than five stamens.

Ask children to make observational drawings of two flowers that they find. For each one, ask: What shape is it? How many stamens does it have?

Pupil Workbook: Complete Activity 2: Comparing flowers on page 54 and Activity 3: Flower tally chart on page 54.

Adaptations and support

Some children will need support to identify the stamens and count them. They may like to take a photograph of the flower. They could either zoom into the image to look closely. Or they could print off the image and circle the parts of the flower on the image.

Take it further

Children could find out about botanists, for example, Ynes Mexia, David Bellamy, Marianne North, Alexander von Humbolt, Harriet Margaret Louise Bolus or Wangari Maathai. Can they find out about a plant discovered or studied by their chosen botanist? Is it a flowering or non-flowering plant? Where was it found?

Reflect and review

Return to the lesson question: **'Do all plants have the same number of reproductive parts?'** Ask children to talk in groups about what they found out. Did they spot any pattern between the number of stamens and the colour or shape of the flower?

Also ask them to explain why counting really tiny things like stamens may help with plant identification.

Answers

The number of stamens in a flower varies in different plants. It varies from one to many per flower but is always the same for a specific plant species. The number is six in the lily family and five in the rose family.

Homework suggestions

Children could find a plant they like – this can be anywhere. But they have to see it in real life! They should look at it for a few minutes and write down a list of describing words or phrases about their plant. They could then draw the leaf and any other important features, such as flower, fruit, pine cone, catkin, bark. Alternatively, they could write a poem about the plant.

They could try to find out the name of the plant. If children can't find its name, they could give the plant a name themselves – something that will help them to remember the plant.

Assessment and evidence of learning

Children can:

- identify, name and describe in detail the function of the reproductive parts of a flower and the processes involved in plant reproduction
- make close observations and compare the number and shape of the reproductive parts of different flowers.

Lesson 3: How can we grow more plants without using seeds?

What children will learn and do

- Children learn that asexual reproduction creates plants that are identical to the parent.
- They grow more plants from cuttings.
- They consider why gardeners use vegetative propagation as a means of growing more plants.
- They answer the lesson question: **'How can we grow more plants without using seeds?'**

This lesson is best taught in the spring and will involve growing plants over the next six to eight weeks.

You will need

For this lesson, you may wish to ask parents/carers, or members of the wider school community, to donate plants and old plant pots. If so, you will need to organise this well in advance.

- plants from which children can propagate new plants:
  - plants with runners; for example, spider plants or strawberry plants
  - plants suitable for taking cuttings; for example, geraniums, fuchsias or pinks
  - plants suitable for splitting: aster, geranium, primula (primrose), salvia
- old plastic plant pots
- compost
- lolly sticks
- scissors
- trowels
- transparent plastic bags
- elastic bands or string
- hormone rooting powder (optional)
- space indoors, well-lit but out of direct sunlight, where children can keep their plant cuttings for the next six to eight weeks

If using the Snap Science Year 5 Pupil Workbook you may not require the resource sheet below.

Snap Science Year 5 Pupil Workbook

- pages 56–57

Snap Science Year 5 Digital subscription

- Slideshow 1: Bramley apples
- Video 1: Plant propagation
- Resource sheet 1: Three ways to propagate plants for the plant sale
- Snapshot 1: Starting all over again

Make sure you have opened/printed any *Snap* resources you intend to use in this lesson.

National Curriculum

Conceptual knowledge:

- describe the life process of reproduction in some plants and animals

Working scientifically:

- reporting and presenting findings from enquiries, including conclusions, causal relationships and explanations of and degree of trust in results, in oral [and written] forms [such as displays and other presentations]

Key vocabulary	
Tier 2 vocabulary:	Tier 3 vocabulary: asexual, propagation, reproduction

Health and safety Please refer to CLEAPSS for Health and Safety guidance and ensure that any identified hazards are managed appropriately.

Green Plant Code

- Always wash your hands after handling plants.
- Remember that some plants can be poisonous or cause allergic reactions in some people. Use gardening gloves if handling plants.
- Do not eat plants you find outside.
- Do not pick wild plants.

Getting started

Remind children that in this module they are studying life cycles. Ask them to recap what they have learnt so far about flowering plant life cycles, prompting them to talk about how seeds are produced from which new plants grow. Remind them, if needed, that seeds are produced when pollen from the male reproductive part of one plant is moved to the female part of another plant of the same type and that this is sexual reproduction).Tell them that in this lesson they are going to learn about how flowering plants can reproduce asexually, through a process called propagation.

Play children Video 1: Plant propagation, which describes how single plants can reproduce themselves, other than by producing seeds. Explain that the gardener will show two methods of vegetative reproduction, where a new plant grows from a fragment of the parent plant or grows from a specialised reproductive structure (such as a stolon, rhizome, tuber, corm or bulb).This is called asexual reproduction because it doesn't need female and male parts from two different plants. Asexual reproduction creates new plants that are identical to the parent plant: they are clones.

Once they have watched the video, ask children to recall the different methods that the gardener uses to grow more plants: stem cuttings, and growing from bulblets. Then talk about other forms of propagation, for example, growing plants from runners, splitting plants or growing new plants from rhizomes or tubers.

Ask: Has anybody propagated plants by taking cuttings, or planted bulbs or grown potatoes themselves?

Encourage children to talk about their experiences of gardening at home or with a relative, or in other classes at school or a gardening club.

Tell children that today they are going to investigate the lesson question: **'How can we grow more plants without using seeds?'**

Pupil Workbook: Complete Activity 1: Plant propagation on page 56.

The task

Tell children that their task is to set up a nursery and grow plants for the school fair. They need to make as many plants as they can. This will involve using vegetative propagation, using existing plants to make more plants. Ensure that all children have access to parent plants from which they can propagate, using at least one of the methods on Resource sheet 1: Propagating plants for the plant sale, (place a copy on each table or display on a screen), old plant pots, lolly sticks for making labels, compost and rooting powder.

Ask children to wash and dry their plant pots before they use them. Ask them to think about why they need to be clean. (Gardeners clean their equipment to minimise the spread of disease between plants.)

Pupil Workbook: Complete Activity 2: Growing plants without seeds on page 56.

Adaptations and support

Some children will need support to prepare their cuttings.

Take it further

Children could try other types of plant propagation, for example, growing garlic from bulbs or potatoes from tubers.

Reflect and review

Ask for a volunteer to explain how to take stem cuttings. Ask: What tips or hints could we add to the instructions on the resource sheet? Repeat for the other two propagation methods.

Return to the lesson question: How can we grow more plants without using seeds? Ask: Do the annotated instruction sheets answer the question? How is propagating plants different to growing them from seeds? Confirm that children understand that propagation involves a single plant, so is an asexual form of reproduction and produces identical plants to the parent plant.

Show children Slideshow 1: Bramley apples. Ask children if they have ever eaten a Bramley apple pie. Tell them that all Bramley apples originate from just one tree.

Explain the following: The tree was grown from an apple pip (seed) by Mary Anne Brailsford between 1809 and 1815. It is thought that it came from an apple grown on a tree at the bottom of her garden in (75 Church Street, Southwell, Nottinghamshire). By 1837, when Mr. Matthew Bramley lived in the house, the tree was producing very fine apples. A local gardener, Henry Merryweather, asked Mr Bramley for permission to take cuttings from the tree. He named the plants that grew from the cuttings the Bramley Seedling.

Ask: Why did they grow lots of this one tree? How might they have done it? Ask: Why do gardeners like to propagate their favourite plants? Children might discuss the following: how gardeners can propagate crops they know are likely to be successful; how it's easier to sell varieties everyone knows and likes, how gardeners can select varieties which are less likely to get disease, will crop well or always look a certain way.

Homework suggestions

Children could take a close look at the plants growing between the cracks in your paving or around the edge of where they live, draw some of these plants and find out their names, if possible. How do they think they got there? Did they get there as a result of pollination or asexual reproduction? Explain their thinking.

Assessment and evidence of learning

Children can:

- describe ways in which plants are able to reproduce other than by producing seeds
- suggest why it is useful for plants to reproduce asexually
- improve a set of instructions for different vegetative propagation methods.

If you are unsure if a child can explain the life process of reproduction in some plants, you can use Snapshot 1: Starting all over again to check understanding and develop learning.

Lesson 4: How do birds change over their lifetime?

What children will learn and do

- Children revisit previous learning about birds.
- They learn that birds lay eggs with hard shells, and that these may or may not be fertilised.
- They observe the inside of an egg.
- They research the life cycle of a chicken and represent it in a diagram.
- They answer the lesson question: **'How do birds change over their lifetime?'**

You will need

- mini whiteboards and pens
- an uncooked chicken egg
- shallow dish
- visualiser (if available)
- access to the internet to show a video of free range chickens

If using the Snap Science Year 5 Pupil Workbook you may not require the resource sheet below.

Snap Science Year 5 Pupil Workbook

- pages 58–59

Snap Science Year 5 Digital subscription

- Video 1: Birds as animals
- Resource sheet 1: Chicken research cards

Make sure you have opened/printed any *Snap* resources you intend to use in this lesson.

National Curriculum

Conceptual knowledge:

- describe the [differences in] the life cycles of a [mammal, an amphibian, an insect and] a bird

Working scientifically:

- recording data and results of increasing complexity using scientific diagrams and labels, [classification keys, tables, scatter graphs, bar and line graphs]

Key vocabulary	
Tier 2 vocabulary:	**Tier 3 vocabulary:** bird, embryo, female, fertilisation, hatch, life cycle, male, mate, organism, vertebrate

Health and safety Please refer to CLEAPSS for Health and Safety guidance and ensure that any identified hazards are managed appropriately.

Getting started

Start by checking on the plant cuttings that children set up in Lesson 3. Ensure that the soil is damp. Discuss any changes that children observe.

Remind children that this module is all about life cycles. Ask: What sort of life cycles have we found out about so far? (Plants.) Tell children that in today's lesson they will start to look at animal life cycles, beginning with birds, one of the vertebrate groups.

Play Video 1: Birds as animals. Tell children that there are around 10,000 different species of birds in the world and almost 600 in Great Britain. Ask: What do you know about birds? Working in pairs, children have two minutes to write down as many key characteristics of birds as they can. Discuss as a class to create a master list of bird features. Play 'True or false' to elicit what children already know about birds. For this game, children need a mini whiteboard. Ask them to write 'true' on one side and 'false' on the other. Read out each of the following statements, asking children to show their answers using their whiteboards.

- All birds can fly. FALSE – There are several birds that cannot fly. These include penguins, kakapo, cassowary, kiwi, steamer ducks and ostriches.
- All birds build nests. FALSE – For example, guillemots lay their eggs on bare rock.
- Birds' nests are always made from sticks. FALSE – For example, gannets build their nests from seaweed, and housemartin nests are made from mud.
- All birds lay eggs. TRUE – Bird eggs have a hard shell and are found in a variety of shapes, sizes and colours.
- Some birds nest underground. TRUE – For example, puffins nest in burrows on grassy cliffs. Sandmartins nest in tunnels in sandy cliffs.

Tell the children that they are going to find out more about chickens, a type of bird, who are kept on farms and sometimes in peoples gardens to provide eggs which are eaten as part of a human diet.

Ask if anyone knows anyone who keeps chickens and if they can share any knowledge about why they have chickens and how they look after them. Show children an online or downloaded video of free range chickens in a farm or domestic setting. What do the children notice about how they move, what they eat, etc?

Explain the following: A hen begins to lay eggs when she is 20 weeks old. From then on she lays one egg a day and may lay over 300 eggs a year. Tell the children that a hen does not actually need to mate with a cockerel to lay eggs. The eggs we eat are unfertilised eggs.

For an egg to develop into a chick, the hen and cockerel mate. Sperm from the male fertilises the egg inside the female's body. If fertilised, an embryo grows inside the egg which contains all the nutrition that is needed before the chick is ready to hatch. Ensure children understand that both hens and cockerels are chickens, but hens are female and cockerels (or roosters) are male.

Show children an uncooked chicken's egg. Ask: What do you think is inside the egg? Crack the egg into a shallow dish. Use a visualiser to help the children to see and identify the following different parts.

- Shell – This is a hard, protective covering made of calcium carbonate. The shell is porous and allows air into the egg and carbon dioxide out.
- Membrane – Eggs have two membranes lining the shell which protect the contents of the egg from bacteria and prevent moisture from leaving the egg too quickly.
- Air cell – Between the membranes is a small air cell, also called an air sac, filled with oxygen. As the chick develops it uses the oxygen from the air cell.
- Albumen – The albumen (egg white) provides the liquid in which the embryo develops, which helps protect it and also contains a large amount of the protein necessary for proper development.
- Chalaza – In a fresh egg, it is possible to see white cords attached to either side of the yolk sac. The chalazae hold the yolk in the centre of the egg.
- Yolk – The yolk is the source of food for the embryo and contains all the fat in the egg.
- Germinal disc – The small spot on the yolk is called the germinal disc. The germinal disc is what would grow into the chick if it was fertilised. If the egg has not been fertilised, you will see a solid spot. If the germinal disc looks like a circle, then the egg was fertilised.

Tell children that today's lesson question is: **'How do birds change over their lifetime?'**

Pupil Workbook: Complete Activity 1: Inside an egg on page 58.

The task

Explain that children are going to find out about the life cycle of a chicken. Tell them that a life cycle includes all the different stages for an organism throughout its life.

Children work in pairs. They draw a circle on a large piece of paper and using Resource sheet 1: Chicken research cards create a life cycle diagram of a chicken, including the different stages in the right order, sticking the pictures in the right places and adding key information from the cards. You could cut these out before and give each pair a set.

Pupil Workbook: Complete Activity 2: Life cycle of a chicken on page 59.

Adaptations and support

Provide a pre-drawn life cycle with five boxes for the children to complete.

Take it further

Ask children to find out about another type of bird's egg and to make a fact file. How many eggs are laid at a time? How big are they? What colour are they? How long are the eggs incubated for?

Alternatively, they could find out which is the smallest bird's egg and the largest bird's egg.

Reflect and review

Ask children to share their chicken life cycles with each other. Do they agree with the order and the key facts?

Return to the lesson question: **'How do birds change over their lifetime?'** In pairs, look at just the chick and adult chicken cards. How are the pictures different? They should notice that the hen has a bright red comb and wattle, adult feathers, scaly legs, and longer tail feathers, whereas the chick is smaller, has downy feathers and a small, pale comb.

Finish with an 'Chicken Eggspert Quiz'. Ask children to use their mini whiteboards again, and hold up 'true' or 'false' when you read out each statement:

- Chicks usually hatch on day 13. FALSE – They hatch on day 21.
- Chicks chip their way out of the egg using their egg tooth. TRUE
- The cockerel sits on the clutch of eggs. FALSE – It is the hen that broods the eggs.
- All chickens are hens. FALSE – Only female chickens are hens. Male chickens are cockerels.
- A pullet is a teenage female hen. TRUE
- An average chicken lifespan is between five and ten years. TRUE
- An egg must be fertilised for a chick to develop. TRUE

Answers

Key features of birds: vertebrate, warm blooded, have feathers, a beak with no teeth, wings, produce hard eggs.

Chicken life cycle:

- Stage 1: Fertilisation
- Stage 2: Incubating (egg)
- Stage 3: Hatching (chick)
- Stage 4: Pullet (teenager)
- Stage 5: Hen/cockerel (adult chicken)

Homework suggestions

Children could choose from one of these activities:

1. Get birdwatching! Sit in a quiet place, by a window or outside. Watch and see how many birds you can spot in ten minutes. Draw a picture of a bird that you spotted. Make notes: Where was it? How big was it? What was it doing?
2. Find out about a famous ornithologist such as Luis Batista, David Lindo, Dr Mya-Rose Craig or Chris Packham.

Assessment and evidence of learning

Children can:

- describe the common characteristics of different types of birds
- sequence the life cycle stages of a chicken
- select and sequence key information to create a life cycle of a chicken.

Lesson 5: Do all mammals have the same gestation period?

What children will learn and do

- Children revisit previous learning about mammals.
- They compare the life cycles of four mammals.
- They look for a pattern between the gestation period of different mammals and their adult weight.
- They compare the life cycle of a mammal with the life cycle of a bird.
- They answer the lesson question: **'Do all mammals have the same gestation period?'**

You will need

- access to reference books or the internet to research gestation periods and adult weights of different mammals
- access to reference books or the internet to research the life cycles of kangaroos and duck billed platypuses (optional)

If using the Snap Science Year 5 Pupil Workbook you may not require all the resource sheets below.

Snap Science Year 5 Pupil Workbook

- pages 60–62

Snap Science Year 5 Digital subscription

- Resource sheet 1: Mammal fact sheet
- Video 1: Marvellous mammals
- Resource sheet 2: Vocabulary match cards
- Resource sheet 3: Gestation table
- Resource sheet 4: Life cycle comparisons

Make sure you have opened/printed any *Snap* resources you intend to use in this lesson.

National Curriculum

Conceptual knowledge:

- describe the differences in the life cycles of a mammal, [an amphibian, an insect and a bird]
- describe the life process of reproduction in some plants and animals

Working scientifically:

- recording data and results of increasing complexity using [scientific diagrams and labels, classification keys, tables, scatter graphs], bar[and line] graphs
- reporting and presenting findings from enquiries, including conclusions, causal relationships [and explanations of and degree of trust in results, in oral and written forms such as displays and other presentations]

Scientific enquiry type:

- pattern seeking

Key vocabulary	
Tier 2 vocabulary:	**Tier 3 vocabulary:** pattern embryo, female, fertilisation, mammal, gestation, life cycle, male, mate, reproduction

Health and safety Please refer to CLEAPSS for Health and Safety guidance and ensure that any identified hazards are managed appropriately.

Getting started

Start by checking on the plant cuttings that children set up in Lesson 3. Ensure that the soil is damp. Discuss any changes that children observe.

Ask children to tell you which life cycles they have studied so far in the module. (Plants and birds.) Tell them that today they are going to find out about the life cycle of various mammals. Ask children to list the key features of a mammal (ask them to think back to Year 4 Module 6, Classification of plants and animals).

Give each child a copy of Resource sheet 1: Mammal detective sheet. Find out what they already know about these animals – African elephant, bat, polar bear and mountain gorilla.

Play Video 1: Marvellous mammals. Ask children to take notes about each animal on their mammal detective sheets as they watch. They will need to gather clues from the images as well as from the voiceover. At the end, ask children to discuss in groups what they learnt about each of the animals. Ask: How are their life cycles similar or different? They may notice that the mountain gorilla has the longest life span, living 50 years; the gorillas are born with fur.

Explain the following: Most mammals have very simple life cycles. Two parent animals mate. The eggs inside the female are fertilised by sperm from the male. This results in an embryo which grows and develops, usually inside the mother. This time between egg fertilisation and giving birth is called the gestation period. When the animal is ready, it is born, and grows from young into an adult.

Give children the cards cut out from Resource sheet 2: Vocabulary match cards. Ask them to put the four terms in sequence (mating, fertilisation, gestation, embryo). Then ask them to match each term with its definition.

Pupil Workbook: Complete Activity 1: Mammals fact sheet on page 60.

The task

Tell children that today they are going to investigate the lesson question: **'Do all mammals have the same gestation period?'**

Ask children to predict which of the following mammals has the longest gestation period: pipistrelle bat, African elephant, mountain gorilla or polar bear.

Ask children to use secondary sources to find out the gestation periods for these four animals and to complete the data on Resource sheet 3: Gestation table.

Then ask children to draw a bar chart, plotting the name of the animal and the length of gestation. In the table on Resource sheet 3, the animals are already in order of weight. This is the order that children should record the data on the bar chart so that the weight of the animal increases from the lightest to the heaviest.

If the children have already learnt to plot points on a scatter graph they can use this method to handle the data.

Pupil Workbook: Complete Activity 2: Gestation periods in mammals on page 61 and Activity 3: Gestation periods in mammals bar chart on page 61.

Adaptations and support

Some children will need a template to draw the bar graph with axes labelled and scale added.

Take it further

Ask children to use secondary sources of information to find out about kangaroos and duck billed platypuses. Their research should focus on how the life cycles of these mammals are different to the animals they have looked at so far in this lesson.

Reflect and review

Return to the lesson question: **'Do all mammals have the same gestation period?'** Ask children if they recognise any pattern between the size of the adult animal and the length of time it takes for the animal to gestate. They should recognise that there is a positive correlation between average adult weight and length of gestation in mammals. Larger mammals are more likely to produce well-developed young than smaller mammals.

Ask: Are there any animals that do not follow that pattern? The children may notice that the tiny pipistrelle bat takes as long as a grey squirrel to gestate, even though the pipistrelle is much smaller. Ask children to research how developed each of those animals are when they are born, and which one is ready to look after itself soonest after birth.

To compare the life cycle of a mammal with a bird life cycle, ask the children to complete Resource sheet 4: Life cycle comparisons. Children should notice the following: Mammals gestate inside the mother while birds develop in an egg outside the mother. Only mammals feed milk to their young. Talk about the differences, and ensure that children recognise that both life cycles are examples of sexual reproduction.

Pupil Workbook: Complete Activity 4: Life cycles of birds and mammals on page 62.

Answers

What is a mammal? Mammals are vertebrates. Mammal mothers give birth to live young and produce milk to feed their babies. Most mammals have four legs or two arms and two legs, but not all mammals live on land: mammals that spend their whole life cycle in aquatic environments have developed fins and flippers. Dogs, cows, elephants, mice, whales and humans are all mammals.

Resource sheet 2: Vocabulary match cards

- Mating – When a male and female animal come together to reproduce.
- Fertilisation – When a male sperm joins a female egg and fertilises it.
- Gestation period – For mammals, this is the time between egg fertilisation and giving birth.
- Embryo – An animal in the early stages of development (in mammals embryos develop inside the mother).

Resource sheet 4: Life cycle comparisons

- Does sperm from the male fertilise eggs inside the female? Mammals YES; Birds YES
- Do eggs develop into embryos inside the female? Mammals YES; Birds YES
- Do eggs develop outside the female? Mammals NO; Birds YES
- Do the young feed on milk from their mother? Mammals YES; Birds NO

Take it further

Kangaroos are marsupials. Female kangaroos remain pregnant for just one month after mating. They give birth to a baby kangaroo called a joey. When it is born, the joey is not fully developed; it is hairless and blind. It makes its way up into the mother's pouch, using its sense of smell. The joey stays there for at least another six months, feeding on its mother's milk. During this time it develops fur, its eyes open and it grows bigger. Even when joeys are large enough to leave the pouch, they still use it for protection and they rely on their mother's milk for over a year.

Duck billed platypuses belong to the monotreme family. Monotremes are different from other mammals because they lay eggs and have no teats. A month after mating, monotremes lay eggs in nursery burrows, where they usually lay two small leathery eggs. The female curls around the eggs and incubates them for another six to ten days. Each tiny platypus hatches from the egg with the aid of an egg tooth. Just like other mammals, duck billed platypuses feed milk to their young, but through milk patches rather than nipples.

Homework suggestions

Children could research and create a fact file about an endangered mammal. This should include why this mammal is under threat and what can be done to save it.

Assessment and evidence of learning

Children can:

- describe the features mammals
- use secondary sources to find out more about the life cycles of different mammals
- compare the life cycle of a mammal with the life cycle of a bird.

Lesson 6: How do amphibians change throughout their life cycle?

What children will learn and do

- Children revisit previous learning about amphibians.
- Children sequence the life cycle of a common frog.
- They research the differences between tadpoles and adult common frogs.
- They discuss the importance of frogs in the wider ecosystem.
- They compare amphibian and bird life cycles.
- They answer the lesson question: **'How do amphibians change throughout their life cycle?'**

You will need

- access to reference books or the internet to research tadpoles and frogs (optional)

If using the Snap Science Year 5 Pupil Workbook you may not require all the resource sheets below.

Snap Science Year 5 Pupil Workbook

- pages 63–64

Snap Science Year 5 Digital subscription

- Video 1: Garden frogs
- Resource sheet 1: Common frog life cycle cards
- Resource sheet 2: Common frog life cycle comparison chart
- Resource sheet 3: Common frog food chains (optional)
- Resource sheet 4: Spot the difference (optional)

Make sure you have opened/printed any *Snap* resources you intend to use in this lesson.

National Curriculum

Conceptual knowledge:

- describe the differences in the life cycles of a mammal, an amphibian, an insect and a bird
- describe the life process of reproduction in some plants and animals

Working scientifically:

- reporting and presenting findings from enquiries, [including conclusions, causal relationships and explanations of and degree of trust in results], in oral and written forms such as displays and other presentations

Key vocabulary	
Tier 2 vocabulary:	**Tier 3 vocabulary:** amphibian, bird, fertilisation, life cycle, metamorphosis

Health and safety Please refer to CLEAPSS for Health and Safety guidance and ensure that any identified hazards are managed appropriately.

Getting started

Start by checking on the plant cuttings that children set up in Lesson 3. Ensure that the soil is damp. Discuss any changes that children observe.

Ask children to tell you which life cycles they have studied so far in the module. (Plants, birds and mammals.) Tell them that today they will be exploring the life cycles of some amphibians.

Ask children to work in pairs. Give them two minutes to make a list of anything they can remember about amphibians (ask them to think back to Year 4 Module 6, Classification of plants and animals). Ask: Can you name any amphibians? Can you remember what all amphibians have in common? How are they different from other animals we have studied in this module?

Tell children that in this lesson they will be using the word 'metamorphosis'. Explain that this is what happens when the young body of an animal goes through huge changes to become an adult. Ask if they know any other animals undergo metamorphosis. Children may remember that other amphibians and some insects such as butterflies go through this process too.

Tell children that today they are going to investigate the lesson question: **'How do amphibians change throughout their life cycle?'**

The task

Play Video 1: Garden frogs.

Ask: Where do frog eggs come from? (They are laid by the female frog.) Where are the eggs fertilised – inside the frog or in the water? Remind children that the female frog lays the eggs in the water and the male frog sprays sperm over the eggs. So they are fertilised in the water. This is different to birds and mammals, whose eggs are fertilised inside the female.

Give each group a set of cards cut out from Resource sheet 1: Common frog life cycle cards. Ask them to work together to place the cards in a life cycle formation.

Discuss how the common frog is different at each stage: egg – tadpole – tadpole with back legs – tadpole with four legs – froglet – frog.

Then ask children to complete Resource sheet 2: Common frog life cycle comparison chart (version A). Children may need to use secondary sources to help them to add detail to their answers.

Pupil Workbook: Complete Activity 1: Common frog life cycle on page 63.

Adaptations and support

Some children may need support to look for the differences between the different stages of the frog life cycle. Provide Resource sheet 2: Common frog life cycle comparison chart (version B).

Take it further

Give children Resource sheet 3: Common frog food chains.

1. Tadpole food chain Ask: which animal might eat the tadpoles? If there are fewer newts what may happen to the number of tadpoles who reach adulthood? What may happen if there is less algae for the tadpoles to eat?
2. Then discuss the frog food chain: leaves→ snail → adult frog → heron. Ask: What happens to the adult frogs if there are fewer snails to eat? What happens to the number of tadpoles the following season? What would happen to the number of adult frogs if there were fewer herons?

Reflect and review

Remind children of the lesson question: **'How do amphibians change throughout their life cycle?'**

Talk through children's comparisons of tadpoles and frogs. Ask: How are they visually different? How is their diet different? How is where they live different? How do their bodies change over time?

Ask children who completed the Food chain activities to explain to the others what they learnt. Ask everyone to think about how frogs are part of more than one food chain?

Explain the following: The fact that frogs go through a process of metamorphosis in their life cycle and live in water and on land greatly increases the range of predators that depend on them for food. This also means that frogs are important animals known as indicator species. They are extremely sensitive to changes in the environment and can give scientists valuable insight into how an ecosystem is functioning. Ask the children to think about how they could create more spaces for frogs in your school grounds.

Ask children to think about what they learnt about chicken and other birds' life cycles in the last lesson. How is a frog life cycle similar to or different from a chicken life cycle. Ensure that children recognise that both frogs and chickens lay eggs, but frogs lay soft eggs in water while chickens lay hard eggs on land.

Pupil Workbook: Complete Activity 2: Comparing tadpoles and frogs on page 64.

Answers

What are amphibians? Amphibians are vertebrates. They are small, cold-blooded animals.. They live on land as well as in the water. They lay soft, jelly-like eggs, usually in or near water. They have moist, smooth skin which helps them to absorb oxygen. Frogs, toads, newts and salamanders are examples of amphibians.

Resource sheet 1: Frog life cycle cards

1. Mating
2. Eggs
3. Tadpole
4. Tadpole with back legs
5. Tadpoles with four legs
6. Froglet
7. Frog

Tadpole and frog comparisons: Tadpoles have no legs when they hatch, then gradually grow back legs followed by front legs. They have a tail that becomes shorter over time. Their eyes are on the sides of their head. An adult frog has four legs, no tail, and its eyes are on top of its head. Tadpoles eat algae, then move on to plants and small insects. Adult frogs eat larger insects, worms, slugs and snails. Tadpoles live in water. Adult frogs live both on the land and in water. Tadpoles breathe using gills, but they also have developing lungs. Adult frogs breathe using lungs.

Homework suggestions

Children could find out about toads and axolotls using Resource sheet 4: Spot the difference.

Ask them to write a list of the differences between an adult axolotl and an adult toad.

Assessment and evidence of learning

Children can:

- describe the common characteristics of different types of amphibian
- sequence the life cycle stages of a common frog
- compare the differences between tadpoles and frogs.

Lesson 7: Do all insects go through the same life cycle?

What children will learn and do

- Children revisit previous learning about insects.
- They observe or research insect life cycles, making observational drawings and noting any changes.
- They learn the difference between complete metamorphosis and incomplete metamorphosis.
- They answer the lesson question: **'Do all insects go through the same life cycle?'**

If using the 'observing over time' option, this lesson is best started in March/April and could take up to three months to complete. Please note that, if you choose to buy stick insect eggs, the stick insects should not be released into the wild when they hatch, as they are a non-native species. Homes will need to be found for these, or they will need to be cared for as class pets.

You will need

- access to reference books and the internet to research insects
- materials for making posters (optional)
- materials for making 3D models (optional)
- digital cameras (optional)
- access to reference books or the internet to research Maria Sibylla Merian, Sophie Lutterlough or Lucy Evelyn Cheesman (optional)

If carrying out the observing over time enquiry, you will need:

- butterfly eggs, net and food – available from companies such as Insectlore
- stick insect eggs, net and food – available from companies such as Insectlore
- digital cameras (optional)

If using the Snap Science Year 5 Pupil Workbook you may not require all the resource sheets below.

Snap Science Year 5 Pupil Workbook

- pages 65–66

Snap Science Year 5 Digital subscription

- Video 1: Insects galore!
- Slideshow 1: Insect life cycles
- Resource sheet 1: Insect observation sheet (optional)
- Resource sheet 2: Insect detective list (optional)
- Snapshot 1: What is the same and what is different?

Make sure you have opened/printed any *Snap* resources you intend to use in this lesson.

National Curriculum

Conceptual knowledge:

- describe the differences in the life cycles of a mammal, an amphibian, an insect and a bird

Working scientifically:

- recording data and results of increasing complexity using scientific diagrams and labels, classification keys, tables, scatter graphs, bar and line graphs

Scientific enquiry type:

- research using secondary sources (or observing over time)

Key vocabulary	
Tier 2 vocabulary:	**Tier 3 vocabulary:** exoskeleton, insect, larva, life cycle, metamorphosis, pupa, reproduction, thorax

Health and safety Please refer to CLEAPSS for Health and Safety guidance and ensure that any identified hazards are managed appropriately.

Invertebrate Codes

- Remember: invertebrates are living creatures. Be very gentle if handling them.
- Don't pick up invertebrates with your fingers. Instead, carefully use a soft paint brush. Place them gently into a collecting pot.
- Keep your invertebrates in the shade and don't leave them in the collecting pot for too long.
- Only put one creature in a collecting pot at a time.
- When you are finished, always return your invertebrate back to the same spot as you found it.
- If you turn over a rock or a log to see what's underneath, always turn it back.

Getting started

Start by checking on the plant cuttings that children set up in Lesson 3. Ensure that the soil is damp. Discuss any changes that children observe.

Ask children to tell you which life cycles they have studied so far in the module. (Plants, birds, mammals and amphibians.) Tell them that today they will be exploring the life cycles of some insects.

Give children two minutes to draw and label an insect of their choice, which shows in as much detail as possible what they already know. After the two minutes have passed, allow them to look at other children's drawings and give them another two minutes to 'magpie' any good ideas that they see.

Play Video 1: Insects galore! Remind children to watch carefully and to remember any additional information to add to their labelled drawing.

Ask: What did you learn that you didn't know already? What additional information do you need to add to your labelled drawing? Then ask children to share their pictures with a partner. Ask them to discuss and agree what features all insects have.

Tell children that today they are going to investigate the lesson question: **'Do all insects go through the same life cycle?'**

The task

Display Slideshow 1: Young and old pictures. First look at the caterpillar and butterfly on slide 1. Tell children the following: Caterpillars are born looking very different to butterflies (the adults of the species). Caterpillars are butterfly larvae. This is their immature larva stage. They will undergo complete metamorphosis and look very different as adults. Ask children to work in pairs to write a list of differences between the caterpillar and the butterfly. What changes in this part of their life cycle?

Then show children the stick insect nymph and stick insect adult on slide 2. Tell children the following: Stick insects are born looking like small versions of their parents. This is an example of insects who undergo incomplete metamorphosis. Ask children to write a list of how the stick insect nymph and adult are the same or different.

Research option:

Ask children to use reference sources to answer the following questions about butterflies and stick insects:

- What are their eggs like?
- How long do the eggs take to hatch?
- What comes out of the egg?
- Do they have a pupa stage?
- Do the adults look like the young?
- Do they go through complete or incomplete metamorphosis?
- What other insects undergo complete metamorphosis?
- What other insects undergo incomplete metamorphosis?

In groups, children make a poster, 3D model or a vlog comparing the two life cycles and listing the other insects they have found out about.

Observation over time option:

If you choose to carry out this observing over time enquiry, children will be able to observe first hand two types of insect (butterflies and stick insects) going through their life cycles into adulthood. The children will need to ensure that the eggs are kept at the optimum temperature, humidity and conditions so that they hatch. Then they need to ensure they provide the correct amount of food and water for the young insects as they grow.

The children will observe how the insects change over the next few weeks, noting these down either in their books or using Resource sheet 1: Insect observation sheet. They need to keep careful records as at the end of the process they will look back to compare examples of complete metamorphosis and incomplete metamorphosis in action.

Questions to consider about each insect:

- What are their eggs like?
- How long do the eggs take to hatch?
- What comes out of the egg?
- Do they have a pupa stage?
- Do the adults look like the young?
- Do they go through complete or incomplete metamorphosis?

The process takes about three months in total and the butterflies will be fully developed before the stick insects. When they emerge from their pupae, the butterflies should be released immediately. The stick insects should not be released into the wild; these will need to be cared for as class pets.

Pupil Workbook: Complete Activity 1: Young and old on page 65 and Activity 2: Comparing insect life cycles on page 66.

Adaptations and support

For the 'observing over time' option, some children may find making observational drawings difficult and may prefer to take regular photographs instead, or keep a video diary.

Take it further

Ask children to find out about an entomologist: either Maria Sibylla Merian, Sophie Lutterlough or Lucy Evelyn Cheesman. How did they work scientifically to learn more about the life cycles of insects?

Reflect and review

Remind children of today's lesson question: **'Do all insects go through the same life cycle?'**

Ask children to share what they have found out about how each type of insect changes over time.

If children have not already discovered this during their research, explain that females stick insects can produce young without needing a male! The eggs she produces are unfertilised, but they develop properly and grow into an adult female stick insect. This is called parthenogenesis, and it is a form of asexual reproduction. If stick insect eggs are fertilised, they could turn out to be male or female.

Display slide 3: Comparing insect life cycles to support children to compare the life cycles of a butterfly and a stick insect. Focus on the similarities and differences between the two animals. Ask: Which animal changes most dramatically over its life cycle? Which one goes through complete metamorphosis and which one incomplete metamorphosis?

Answers

What is an insect? Insects are invertebrates. They are small animals with a hard covering over their bodies, which is known as an exoskeleton (this is a skeleton, but it is on the outside of their bodies). Insects have a body that is divided into three parts: head, thorax and abdomen. Most insects also have three pairs of legs and one or two pairs of wings. They have a pair of feelers on their heads, called antennae.

What is complete metamorphosis? Complete metamorphosis includes four stages: egg, larva, pupa and adult. During the pupa phase, the insect's body is completely rebuilt and transformed so that the adult insect looks completely different from the larva, and may well eat different foods. Examples include butterflies, moths, beetles, bees, wasps, ants and flies.

What is incomplete metamorphosis? Incomplete metamorphosis includes three stages: egg, nymph and adult. When the young hatch they look like the adults but are smaller and do not have wings. Examples include stick insects, true bugs, dragonflies, grasshoppers and earwigs.

What is an instar? Insects go through five instars. An instar is the developmental stage of an insect between moults. For example, after hatching from the egg, an insect is said to be in its first instar. When the insect moults it is then a second instar and so on.

Homework suggestions

Children can use Resource sheet 2: Insect detective list to help them find evidence of insects near where they live or in the school grounds. They may find eggs laid on the underside of a leaf, caterpillars, larvae, pupae, adult insects, nymphs or signs of insect life such as scale insects, holes in leaves, large holes in Leaves, leaves curling up, sticky honeydew (- excreted by aphids), cuckoo spit - (a white frothy liquid secreted by the nymphs of froghoppers), a bee on a flower, ant eggs underneath a rock, insects caught in a spider's web. Children should take photographs or draw pictures, noting the type of insect and which plants they find them on.

Assessment and evidence of learning

Children can:

- describe the common characteristics of different types of insect
- describe the differences and similarities between two different types of insect life cycles
- use reference sources to gather information OR record observation data over time in drawing and text.

If you are unsure if a child can describe the differences in the life cycles of a mammal, an amphibian, an insect and a bird, you can use Snapshot 1: What is the same and what is different? to check understanding and develop the learning.

Module 5: Separating mixtures and changing materials

Lesson 1: How can we separate mixtures?

What children will learn and do

- Children learn that materials can be mixed in different ways.
- They learn that mixtures can be separated.
- They make their own sieves to separate a mixture of dry solids.
- They communicate the process they have used using a flowchart or diagram.
- They answer the lesson question: **'How can we separate mixtures?'**

You will need

- disposable plates of different kinds (such as paper, cardboard, foil, bamboo – avoid single use plastic where possible) – these can be pierced (carefully) with nails, hole punches or skewers to form makeshift sieves
- selection of fabrics, nets and gauzes
- 'Cupboard Catastrophe' mixture (use out of date foodstuffs where possible) – rice, raisins, large pasta, flour, dried lentils, dried peas, fine sand, white sugar, metal paper clips, wood shavings, plus three or four toy spiders
- large foil trays
- magnets
- spoons

If using the Snap Science Year 5 Pupil Workbook you may not require the resource sheet below.

Snap Science Year 5 Pupil Workbook

- pages 67–68

Snap Science Year 5 Digital subscription

- Resource sheet 1: Sort recording grid (optional)
- Animation 1: The process of milling flour

Make sure you have opened/printed any *Snap* resources you intend to use in this lesson.

National Curriculum

Conceptual knowledge:

- use knowledge of solids, liquids, and gases to decide how mixtures might be separated, including through filtering, sieving and evaporating

Working scientifically:

- reporting and presenting findings from enquiries, including conclusions, causal relationships, and explanations of and degree of trust in results, in oral and written forms such as displays and other presentations

Key vocabulary	
Tier 2 vocabulary: combine/combining, flow chart, grade (of sieve), particle, puncture	**Tier 3 vocabulary:** conclude/conclusion, explain/explanation separate/separating, sieve, solid

Health and safety Please refer to CLEAPSS for Health and Safety guidance and ensure that any identified hazards are managed appropriately.

Getting started

This is the first lesson of the second Year 5 Chemistry module. Ensure that children are given opportunities throughout to consider their learning from the previous module and build their developing conceptual knowledge upon that core content.

To begin with, set up a small demonstration featuring pairs of materials, such as rice and peas, paper clips and small plastic cubes, sugar and sand, gravel and water, salt and water. Encourage children to name the materials they can see and introduce the term mixture, used to describe what is formed when two (or more) dry solid materials, or a liquid and a solid or solids are combined. Ask: What would happen if we mixed these materials together? Do you think it would be possible to separate them again? How might this be done? Select several children to mix the pairs of materials and report back to the rest of the class what appears to happen as the materials combine. Establish that materials combined in a mixture need to be separated in different ways, depending on the types of materials that are mixed. Explain that they will be separating mixtures of solid materials in this lesson. Those involving water will be investigated next lesson.

During this lesson children will use their science skills as they design, make and test sieves to separate a complex mixture. The task itself requires them to be inventive as they problem solve using limited resources, making choices and testing materials to see what works best. They will communicate the process they have used in a flow chart and use it as they draw conclusions and give explanations of what they have learned about how to separate a mixture of dry solids.

Set the scene for the task by presenting children with a box full of debris from a 'Cupboard Catastrophe'. Explain that a shelf has collapsed in the school storeroom (or science cupboard) and several containers (between six and ten) full of solid materials have been tipped out and mixed together. The caretaker, intending to help, has made things worse by sweeping up all the remains, including the odd dead spider, and has put them into this box.

Tell children that the lesson question today is: **'How can we separate mixtures?'** They will answer this as they work out how to sort the mess of materials that the caretaker has left in the box. Show them a sieve and ask for a volunteer to explain how they think it works, demonstrating its use with some of the mixed dry materials from earlier in the lesson. Ask: What is this sieve made of? How does it separate a mixture? Does it work for all these materials? What types of solid is it best used for? Draw children's attention to the size of the holes in the sieve and ask them to suggest materials that might not be separated using this grade of sieve. Unfortunately children from another class are using most of the school's sieves (a very useful piece of equipment that might help with this task) today, so they will need to make their own sieves.

Show children the range of resources that could be used to make a simple sieve, including a variety of disposable plates that might have holes added to them, nets and gauzes. It may be necessary to demonstrate how to use a hole punch, nail, and/or skewer safely. Provide sample materials for children to use as they test out their technique, before they transfer their hole-making to a plate. Children work in pairs or small groups and collaboratively to complete the task; this will limit to an extent the materials needed and used, as well as encourage the sharing of ideas and practical solutions to the task.

Pupil Workbook: Complete Activity 1: Separating mixtures on page 67.

The task

Prompt children to think about the steps they will need to take to separate each 'Cupboard Catastrophe' solid from the mixture and the most effective order for those steps. Remind them once again that solids with different size particles will require a sieve or sieves with different sized holes.

Ask: Are there any materials you can remove easily before you begin sieving? Children should indicate any larger objects (like the spiders) that could be removed using the fingers. Encourage them also to think about any metal objects in the mixture (include an aluminium ring pull or two), as well as the steel paper clips. Ask: What science equipment could be used to separate any metal objects from the mixture?

Check children's understanding of the properties of metals by asking them whether all metal objects in the mixture would be attracted to a magnet.

Once the largest objects and any magnetic metal objects are removed, ask children to think about a sequence for separating the other solid materials. Ask: Which solids will you remove first? Will it be the biggest solids or the smallest? Will you need more than one sieve? Can you adapt a single plate to make an effective set of sieves? Are there any other materials you could use to make a sieve (especially for solids made up of very small particles)? If necessary, prompt them to look at fabrics of different kinds that could work. These might be stretched over a frame or drawn together into a bag.

Ask children to draw a flow chart or diagram to record the order in which they separated the different materials and the equipment they used. Remind them to make notes about each step of the process as they separate the mixture. They will need to use that evidence as they draw conclusions and explain their findings later.

Pupil Workbook: Complete Activity 2: Sorting mixtures on page 68.

Adaptations and support

Children could be given a simpler mixture to separate, containing fewer solid materials. They could also be supported as they make their sieves. For example, give them a paper plate to adapt to act as a sieve. Show them how they could puncture it using a variety of tools to allow solids of different sizes to pass through. They could use Resource sheet 1: Sort recording grid as a means of recording their sort rather than producing a flow chart.

Take it further

Ask children to design a system of sieving using a large foil tray that can separate all the different solids, with their varying particle sizes, from the mixture. They may use additional resources, such as a magnet and some stiff card, to separate out sections of the tray to complete their task. When they have created their super sieve system, they should place each solid in a separate container. Ask children to draw a labelled diagram of the super sieve showing how it is made and what property of the material allows it to be separated by a part of the super sieve.

Reflect and review

Remind children once again of the lesson question: **'How can we separate mixtures?'** Encourage them to think about the mixture they have separated and identify what they have learned about the process. Select flow charts produced and ask children to share their process with another pair or group. Encourage them to report back details of their process. Ask: How did you separate the mixture? How successful was your method? Were all the solids clearly separated? Did you manage to retrieve them all? How many were there? Were there any solids that you could not retrieve using a sieve?

This discussion should reinforce/confirm children's understanding that particles that pass through a sieve are smaller than the holes in the sieve itself. Larger solid particles cannot go through and remain in the sieve. Therefore, sieves can be especially designed to let specific sizes of particles pass through. Prompt children to offer an explanation of how sieves work. Note down main points raised on flipchart or white board.

Show children Animation 1: The process of milling flour illustrating a real-world application of sieving. The miller sieves the flour repeatedly during the process. We are told that at each stage of the milling process flour is removed and bagged up, ready for use in bread making, while other by-products are not wasted but used in different ways by the food industry.

Ask: Why does the unprocessed flour have to be sieved more than once? What happens to the material that does not go through the sieve? Why is it important for the flour to be as fine as possible?

Look once again with the children at their explanations of the sieving process. Encourage them to edit their explanations in the light of what they have just seen and talked about.

Answers

What is a mixture?

Children can explain that a mixture is a combination of materials, made up of either solids or solids mixed with a liquid. They can give examples of mixtures of solids and recognise that the different solids in a mixture have different size particles.

How can a mixture be separated?

Children describe how the process of sieving can be used to separate a complex mixture. They understand that the grade of sieve, the hole size, must be different in order to separate solids with different size particles. They can suggest other methods (at this point), such as using their fingers to remove larger objects or a magnet to retrieve magnetic materials.

How can you adapt a single plate to make an effective set of sieves?

Children can describe that when small holes are made in a plate almost all of the mixture, apart from the finest solids like sand, is stopped from going through. As holes in the plate are made bigger the mixture can be separated, as each bigger solid is allowed through while the biggest are held back.

Homework suggestions

Ask children to look at home for examples of equipment that performs the same function as a sieve. This might include, slotted spoons, kitchen sieves, colanders, garden/building sieves for refining materials in a similar way to that done in the milling process. Tell them to draw an annotated diagram of equipment found, detailing its use in separating mixtures of materials.

Assessment and evidence of learning

Children can:

- explore the behaviour of a mixture, adapting and testing a variety of materials and techniques in order to mechanically separate the mixture
- record evidence of the process used to separate a mixture in a flow chart
- use appropriate vocabulary to describe and explain the processes used to separate a mixture
- explain that the smaller the particle size of a solid to be separated from a mixture, the smaller the holes in a sieve must be
- explain that some solid materials, such as sugar, are impossible to separate entirely by sieving; another method of separation is required
- explain that materials can be separated by using differences in their properties, for example, magnetic metals.

Lesson 2: What happens when we mix liquids and solids?

What children will learn and do

- Children learn that some solids dissolve in liquid water while others do not.
- They test a variety of materials to establish whether they dissolve.
- They record the results of their test in a table.
- They learn that solids which dissolve break down in water to form a solution.
- They describe how they know that a solid has dissolved.
- They answer the lesson question: **'What happens when we mix liquids and solids?'**

You will need

- water, sand, salt, fruit syrup, brown sugar for demo
- filter funnels, filter paper
- reusable transparent beakers
- collection of solids – powder paint, flour, sugar, sand, coffee granules, bath salts, tea leaves, baby powder, sugar substitute, bicarbonate of soda
- beakers, spoons, weighing equipment, measuring jugs
- mini whiteboards or sketchpads

If using the Snap Science Year 5 Pupil Workbook you may not require the resource sheet below.

Snap Science Year 5 Pupil Workbook

- pages 69–70

Snap Science Year 5 Digital subscription

- Resource sheet 1: Do solids dissolve? (one per pair of children) (optional)
- Interactive 1: True/False/Maybe
- Snapshot 1: Separating mixtures

Make sure you have opened/printed any *Snap* resources you intend to use in this lesson.

National Curriculum

Conceptual knowledge:

- know that some materials dissolve in liquid to form a solution, [and describe how to recover a substance from a solution]

Working scientifically:

- using test results to make predictions to set up further comparative [and fair] tests
- planning different types of scientific enquiries to answer questions, including recognising [and controlling] variables, where necessary

Scientific enquiry type:

- identifying and classifying

Key vocabulary	
Tier 2 vocabulary: Particle	**Tier 3 vocabulary:** observe/observation dissolve, evaporate/evaporation, filter, insoluble, saturated, separate/separating, soluble, solution

Health and safety Please refer to CLEAPSS for Health and Safety guidance and ensure that any identified hazards are managed appropriately.

Getting started

Show children the pairs of materials that included water from the last lesson – sand and water, salt and water. Ask them to think about what happened when those materials were mixed. What can they recall? Repeat the mixing of those materials once again for the children as a reminder. This might be done in pairs or as a demonstration. Tell them to watch carefully what happens to each mixture in turn. Can children describe what they see happening? Prompt children to notice what is similar and different about the two mixtures, for example, how both mixtures include water, but in one the solid (sand) remains separate from the water, although mixed into/combined with the water it is insoluble, while in the other the solid salt mixes into the water and cannot be seen.

Ask whether they have any ideas about how they could separate the solids from the water. This can be easily achieved in the case of sand and water by filtering, which is a similar process to sieving (the focus of Lesson 1). Provide children with filter funnels and filter paper and ask them to separate the mixture of sand and water. If necessary, quickly show some or all children how to use this equipment, reminding them of when they may have used it before. Draw their attention to the fact that the water appears clear and free of sand once it has gone through the filter funnel. Wet sand remains in the filter paper. Ask: Why is the sand still wet? What needs to happen to the sand to get it back to how it was before it was mixed with the water? Remind them what they learnt about how water dries using the word evaporate to describe the process of water changing from a liquid to a gas.

Turn to the second mixture. Explain that they need to think a little more about what happened to the solid salt when it was added to the water before they can try to separate it. Introduce the term dissolve to the children. This word is used to describe what happens to some materials when they are added to a liquid. The solid salt crystals, in this case, break down into smaller particles and mix with the liquid water, with no noticeable change of colour.

Ask: Can you think of any other solids that dissolve when they are put into water?

Show children a number of beakers containing water. Mark the level of the water. Ask them to predict what will happen to the level of the water if sand is added to one of the beakers. Ask: What will happen if add fruit syrup instead of sand? What about some brown sugar?

Ask them to draw quickly on a mini whiteboard or sketchpad what they predict will happen to the level of the water and share their responses. Now add similar amounts of each material in turn to separate beakers and mark the new water level (insoluble materials increase the water level, but dissolved solids break down and combine with the water, so that their presence doesn't make a difference to the level of the water on mixing). Are they surprised? Can they explain what they have seen? Revisit children's ideas shared at this point later in the lesson, where relevant.

Tell children that the lesson question today is **'What happens when we mix liquids and solids?'**

As children carry out their task, they will work scientifically using the skills of observation and comparison to determine whether a solid dissolves or not. They will also consider scientific variables that could be changed to explore the behaviour of dissolving solids, for example, what if the mixture were stirred, or the temperature of the water increased?

Pupil Workbook: Complete Activity 1: Soluble and insoluble on page 69.

The task

Show children a selection of solids (see suggestions in resource list) that they might test to discover whether they are soluble or insoluble. Provide a selection of suitable equipment for them to use as they set up their test. Encourage children to work together in groups to plan their test. Remind them, if needed, to consider both the volume of water they will use and the amount of solid that should be added in each case. Tell children to draft a table of results in which to record their observations of each solid and whether it dissolves or not.

Prompt children, once initial observations have been made, to stir the mixture and observe whether that makes a difference. Ask: What did you notice when you first added the water to the solid? Were there any changes straight away? Did all the solid dissolve? Did stirring the solid help?

Pupil Workbook: Complete Activity 2: Dissolving solids on page 69.

Adaptations and support

Children might be given fewer solids to test for solubility and provided with support as they decide on a method to use. For example, show children how to measure out, then place a small amount of one solid in a reusable transparent beaker. Tell them to watch carefully, making observations of any changes that happen as they add a small amount of water to the solid. Provide children with the scaffold of a pre-prepared table, Resource sheet 1: Do solids dissolve? one between two, on which to record their observations, initially in the first column.

Take it further

Ask: How much of a solid can dissolve in a liquid? What would you estimate? Is it the same for each solid?

Introduce the idea that when no more solid can be dissolved into a liquid, the solution is said to be saturated.

The children should compare both salt and sugar, working with no more than 50 ml water and solids to begin with. They should make detailed observations and record the quantities of solid they add systematically.

Ask: How will you know when the solution is saturated? What will you see? What will the solution feel like? Do you think that more or less of the solid would dissolve if the water were hotter? Why?

When they have completed their test, they should draw and label diagrams to explain what has happened.

Reflect and review

Remind children once again of the lesson question: **'What happens when we mix liquids and solids?'** Ask them to summarise what they have learned. Which solids dissolved? How do you know that the solid had dissolved? What happened to those solids that did not dissolve? Some, like flour, baby powder or tea leaves form a suspension, not dissolving but remaining suspended in the water. Introduce the term solution to describe a mixture of water and dissolved solid. Ensure that children recognise that some coloured solids dissolve, resulting in a coloured solution. Some children might think that a solution must be colourless, like the salt and water solution and if they can see a colour change that the material has not dissolved.

Check that children can use newly introduced vocabulary, such as suspension, correctly. Ask children to think about the enquiry type that they have been using today. Ensure that they recognise that they have been 'grouping and classifying things', in this case solids, as either soluble or insoluble.

To explore the children's understanding of the topic at this point use Interactive 1: True/False/Maybe. Display the interactive and ask children to suggest which statement in turn should be placed into which category, justifying their choice each time. Some of the statements cannot be answered directly from the work done in this lesson – note children's answers and reasons and explain that they will investigate these in the next lessons. Do not give the correct answers to this interactive at this stage. It will be revisited in the next lesson.

Answers

What happens when we mix liquids and solids?

Children can explain that different solids behave differently when mixed with liquids. They might share outcomes of their tests observing that some solids do not dissolve and remain in suspension, such as flour, or sink to the bottom of the beaker like sand. Other solids dissolve; these solids break down, combining with the liquid.

What does dissolving mean?

Children can explain in simple terms that a solid which dissolves breaks down into smaller pieces / particles when it comes into contact with a liquid and these particles mix with the liquid forming a solution. They might explain that, for example, particles of dissolved solid cannot be seen, unless the solid is coloured and that the solid, once combined with the liquid, does not cause the level in a beaker to go up (referencing the demonstration activity in 'Getting started') because the particles of solid are so small that they 'hide away' within the water.

Which solids dissolve?

Children can name a number of solids that dissolve and describe whether or not the resulting solution is coloured or not.

How do we know that a solid has dissolved?

Children can explain that a dissolved solid is not visible. They might refer to the need to stir some solids to ensure everything dissolves. Some children who took their learning further may understand that a solution can become saturated and explain, for example, 'there is a limit to how much salt can be dissolved in a small volume of water. If the solution is saturated, crystals of salt stay at the bottom of the beaker and the mixture looks and feels thicker.'

True, False or Maybe?

Children may be able to correctly position (some) True and False statements (see below). Any 'Maybe' responses indicate uncertainty and will be addressed in later teaching, so be careful not to give away answers at this point. Answers here are intended to support teacher subject knowledge only.

True

If you can't dissolve any more solid the liquid is saturated.
Dissolved coloured sugar is dissolved even though you can still see its colour.
Some solids can dissolve in liquids other than water.
Some types of sugar take much longer to dissolve than others.
Some solids don't dissolve, but they don't form a suspension either.
Sugar dissolves more quickly when the water is hot.

False

Some powders dissolve a bit and what's left stays in the water.
You can't get back a dissolved solid.
When water is cold you can't dissolve anything.

Homework suggestions

Children could list examples of dissolving they observe at home, for example when preparing eating food, washing or doing craft activities.

Assessment and evidence of learning

Children can:

- record observations accurately in a table of their own design
- use scientific vocabulary correctly as they describe and explain their observations, for example, use the terms dissolve, solution and suspension appropriately
- explain that some materials dissolve in liquid to form a solution while others do not
- explain that materials which do not dissolve, such as flour, may form a suspension in the water or remain at the bottom of the container like sand

- explain what happens when a solid dissolves in a liquid, recognising that a dissolved solid breaks down and combines with the liquid and that the resulting solution may be coloured rather than colourless.

If you are unsure whether a child knows that some materials dissolve in liquid to form a solution you can use Snapshot 1: Separating mixtures to check understanding and develop their learning.

Lesson 3: What makes a difference to how fast sugar or salt dissolves?

What children will learn and do

- Children learn how the rate at which solids dissolve in liquid water can be changed.
- They plan and carry out a comparative test to explore variables that might affect the rate at which solids dissolve.
- They learn how a dissolved solid can be retrieved from a solution using the process of evaporation.
- They answer the lesson question: **'What makes a difference to how fast sugar or salt dissolves?'**

You will need

- rock salt, table salt, icing sugar, Demerara sugar, granulated sugar, water
- transparent beakers, saucers, teaspoons
- measuring equipment, timers
- hand lenses, mini microscopes

If using the Snap Science Year 5 Pupil Workbook you may not require the resource sheet below.

Snap Science Year 5 Pupil Workbook

- pages 71–73

Snap Science Year 5 Digital subscription

- Lesson 2, Interactive 1: True/False/Maybe
- Resource sheet 1: Does the type of sugar make a difference? (optional)
- Slideshow 1: Dissolving solids discussion
- Snapshot 1: Solutions

Make sure you have opened/printed any *Snap* resources you intend to use in this lesson.

National Curriculum

Conceptual knowledge:

- know that some materials dissolve in liquid to form a solution, and describe how to recover a substance from a solution

Working scientifically:

- planning different types of scientific enquiries to answer questions, including recognising, and controlling variables where necessary
- reporting and presenting findings from enquiries, including conclusions, causal relationships, and explanations of and degree of trust in results, in oral and written forms such as displays and other presentations

Scientific enquiry type:

- comparative testing

Key vocabulary	
Tier 2 vocabulary: room temperature	**Tier 3 vocabulary:** comparative test, predict/prediction, variable dissolve, reversible, saturated, solution

Health and safety Please refer to CLEAPSS for Health and Safety guidance and ensure that any identified hazards are managed appropriately.

Getting started

Use the drag and drop interactive from the previous lesson (Lesson 2, Interactive 1) to remind children of the discussion they had at the end of last lesson and the true/false/maybe statements they discussed.

Ask them to share their ideas about what will make a difference to the time it takes for a solid to dissolve and prompt with further questions, where necessary. Ask: What difference does stirring make? Would the amount of solid make a difference? The volume of liquid used? The shape and size of the pieces of solid? What will happen if we change the temperature of the water to dissolve a solid?

Remind children that the things that might be changed are known as variables.

At this point, encourage children who investigated saturation point as they took their learning further during Lesson 2 to explain that there is a limit to how much solid will dissolve in a given volume of water. The water becomes saturated and no more solid will dissolve. Ask: How did you know that the water was saturated? What did you see?

Tell children that the lesson question today is: **'What makes a difference to how fast sugar and salt dissolves?'** Explain that they will be carrying out a comparative test to investigate variables that might affect the rate at which two solids dissolve in water and make a solution.

Pupil Workbook: Complete Activity 1: Dissolving solids on page 71.

The task

Explain to the children that they need to come up with a method to use to find out what makes the most difference to the time it takes for a solid (either salt or sugar) to dissolve in water. Refer back to the variables identified earlier. Ask: What do you think will make the most difference to the dissolving rate? Why? How will you test your prediction? What equipment will you use? How will you record your results? Prompt groups, if necessary, to construct a table of results to record details relevant to their chosen change variable and the evidence they collect, for example, if temperature is the change variable, a record of a starting water temperature (cold, room temperature, tap hot) and the time taken for the solid to dissolve completely.

Remind them to change only one thing at a time as they investigate, while keeping everything else the same, and choosing either salt or sugar as their focus material. For example, using the same quantity of salt and volume of water, they might change the temperature of the water or the number of stirs or the type of salt. Tell children to complete their tests, remembering to record their results as they work.

Establish across the groups the material being tested and variable being changed. Record this information on a display to use later as children consider what they have found out.

Pupil Workbook: Complete Activity 2: Comparative test: dissolving rate on page 72.

Adaptations and support

Provide a reduced focus, for example, tell children to compare the rate at which sugars of different type, such as icing sugar, Demerara sugar and granulated sugar, dissolve. Ask them to predict which sugar will dissolve quickest and make a note of it on Resource sheet 1: Does the type of sugar make a difference? then use the rest of the grid to record their results.

Explain that they need to come up with a test to compare the time taken for different sugars to dissolve in water at room temperature. If necessary, prompt them with a simple method: Use transparent beakers, the same amount of water and 1 teaspoon of each type of sugar in each beaker.

Tell the children to complete their test. Ask: Did all the sugars dissolve? Which dissolved quickest? Which was the slowest? Why do you think that might be? How could you speed up the process?

Take it further

Provide children with a selection of salt and sugar (of different types and crystal size) to compare. Prompt them by asking questions as they plan. Ask: What do you think will affect the dissolving rate of the solids the most? Children will probably repeat points made earlier, for example, stirring, the temperature of the liquid and the amount of solid. Encourage them to also think about the particle size of each type of solid as, for example, comparing rock salt and caster sugar might distort their evidence. Ask them to suggest why this might be the case. Prompt them, if needed, to think about the crystal sizes of the two solids: the crystals of each have distinctly different surface areas, and this might affect the rate at which the different types of salt dissolve.

Children should plan their comparative test and systematically record their results, including numerical data, in a table they construct as they carry out their investigation.

Reflect and review

Remind children of the lesson question: **'What makes a difference to how fast sugar or salt dissolves?'**

Look at the display where you recorded (at the beginning of the lesson) the name of each group's solid and the variable being changed. Tell children to refer to the evidence they recorded and report back on their investigation. Prompt them to compare outcomes by asking: Which variable seems to have made the solid dissolve fastest? Which do you think had the least effect? Why do you think that is? Encourage children to consider how they might confirm their thinking about what makes the most difference to the dissolving rate and to share their ideas, such as 'We think temperature of water makes the most difference. We could retest the temperature of water for all the materials, so that we can be sure increasing the temperature makes all solids dissolve quicker'.

Linking back to the last lesson, show children Slideshow 1: Dissolving solids discussion. They will see drawings of children discussing their dissolving solids investigation. Introduce the term reversible to describe a material change where the materials involved can change back to their original state. Ask: Do we think that this change is reversible or not? Ask children for feedback. Their responses and explanations will provide useful information about their understanding of how materials can be separated.

Ask one child from each group to pour a small amount of the dissolved salt or sugar solutions from their group's investigation into shallow containers (saucers are ideal). Tell them to leave the containers in different places around the classroom, so that everyone can observe and record any changes that take place in preparation for the next lesson.

Ask them to think about what difference the volume of solution in the saucer will make to the time it takes for the solid to reappear. Children might raise several variables that could also affect the rate of evaporation: the amount of solid dissolved in the solution (its concentration); the temperature of the room; and the position of the saucer in the classroom.

Pupil Workbook: Complete Activity 3: Reflect and review on page 73 and Activity 4: Is this change irreversible? on page 73.

Answers

What makes a difference to how fast sugar or salt dissolves?

Children can suggest a number of factors initially that might affect the rate at which the two solids dissolve. These might include, for example, stirring/shaking, changing the temperature of the water, type of liquid, amount of solid, volume of liquid. They might refer to prior knowledge of the impact that increasing temperature has on speed of melting (Year 4 – States of matter) and say, 'I think that the higher the temperature of the water the faster a solid will dissolve.' They should recognise other variables that might make a difference and explain whether the results of their investigation support their ideas. Following discussion, they should be able to explain that the time taken for a solid to dissolve depends on several variables, including: the size and shape of crystals; amount of stirring; temperature of liquid.

How can a dissolved solid be separated from a mixture?

Children can describe a simple process to retrieve the solid from a solution. They might say, 'If we put a container with salt solution in a sunny place the water will evaporate leaving salt crystals behind.' They can explain that the particles of solid broken down and dissolved in a solution are too small for a filter funnel and paper to be used to remove them.

What kind of change is this?

Children can explain that this is a reversible change. They might say, 'the materials in the mixture, salt and water, can be separated and are still the same. The salt is there even though we can't see it. The water can be evaporated from the solution and the salt will reappear – so it's a reversible change.'

Homework suggestions

No suggested homework is assigned for this lesson.

Assessment and evidence of learning

Children can:

- identify variables that might make a difference to the rate at which a solid dissolves
- plan a comparative investigate their group's question
- collaboratively record evidence in a table of results constructed specifically for their investigation
- discuss evidence collected with other groups as they decide which variables seemed to have had the most impact on the rate of dissolving.
- explain their observations in relation to the specific variable their group changed and its impact on rate of dissolving, for example, that increasing the temperature of the water seems to speed up the dissolving process
- explain which variable explored by all children appears to have had most impact on rate of dissolving, making reference to their evidence of this
- explain that a dissolved solid can be retrieved from a solution by evaporating the liquid to leave the solid behind.

If you are unsure whether a child knows that some materials dissolve in liquid to form a solution you can use Snapshot 1: Solutions to check understanding and develop their learning.

Lesson 4: How can we clean up contaminated water?

What children will learn and do

- Children use their knowledge of separating mixtures to solve a real-world problem.
- They test a variety of materials as filters to clean up contaminated water.
- They learn that water that appears to be 'clean' may still be undrinkable.
- They answer the lesson question: **'How can we clean up contaminated water?'**

You will need

Preparation required in advance of lesson: make a supply of 'contaminated' water – a soupy mixture containing, for example, oil, soil, sand, pebbles, leaves and twigs, bits of plastic, and so on

- children's solutions from last class, which if possible have been left around the classroom
- containers of 'contaminated' water – a soupy mixture containing, for example, oil, soil, sand, pebbles, leaves and twigs, bits of plastic, and so on
- sieves with different grade mesh
- funnels of different sizes, filter papers
- buckets, bowls, waterproof sheeting, mop and bucket
- containers to use for making filters – large plant pots, bucket (punctured), large foil tray (with deep sides), garden sieves
- rock collection for making filter beds – fine sand, coarse sand, fine gravel, coarse gravel, pebbles (around 1 cm in size)
- material collection for making filter beds – wadding, felts and other thick fibrous fabrics
- cameras (optional)
- microscopes
- reference materials for research (optional)

If using the Snap Science Year 5 Pupil Workbook you may not require all the resource sheets below.

Snap Science Year 5 Pupil Workbook

- pages 74–76

Snap Science Year 5 Digital subscription

- Resource sheet 1: Process planner (optional)
- Resource sheet 2: Filter bed instructions (to display)

Make sure you have opened/printed any *Snap* resources you intend to use in this lesson.

National Curriculum

Conceptual knowledge:

- use knowledge of solids, liquids, and gases to decide how mixtures might be separated, including through filtering, sieving and evaporating

Working scientifically:

- reporting and presenting findings from enquiries, including conclusions, causal relationships, and explanations of and degree of trust in results, in oral and written forms such as displays and other presentations

Scientific enquiry type:

- research using secondary sources of information

Key vocabulary	
Tier 2 vocabulary:	**Tier 3 vocabulary:** evidence condense, contamination, crystal/crystalline, dissolve, evaporate/evaporation, filter, reversible, solution

Health and safety Please refer to CLEAPSS for Health and Safety guidance and ensure that any identified hazards are managed appropriately.

Getting started

Begin the lesson by looking at the containers of solution the children put to one side at the end of the last lesson. These were placed in different positions around the classroom.

Ask some of them to share what they noticed. Ensure that discussions make reference to, for example, the fact that the salt or sugar has changed in appearance after being dissolved, the crystalline structure may be more evident; that all the solid has been retrieved – weighing another mixture before and after dissolving and evaporating can be used to address any doubts; that the liquid water from the evaporated solution has become a gas (water vapour) and mixed with the air. Remind children of the term reversible: this change to a solution can be reversed; the materials were not lost or changed permanently. The water evaporated. If the vapour was captured in a closed system and cooled, it would return to a liquid state.

Tell children that the lesson question today is: **'How can we clean up contaminated water?'** Explain that contaminated water is impure or dirty in some way. Impurities might be visible, but often cannot be seen with the naked eye. Ask children to think about what they learned about pollution in Year 4 and to suggest ways in which water can become contaminated. They may suggest sea pollution from sewers, oil and debris from ships; river pollution from chemicals used in farming, field runoff chemicals, discharge from factories, waste material carelessly discarded.

Explain to children that their task today is to use what they have learned already about separating mixtures and come up with a method for cleaning contaminated water.

Pupil Workbook: Complete Activity 1: Separating mixtures on page 74.

The task

Remind children to think back to what they have learned already about sieves, filters and how they work. They will need to share ideas and collaborate in their group to create a series of filter beds that could be used to clean up a contaminated water supply.

As they carry out their task they will work scientifically, applying their knowledge of scientific processes to solve a problem.

Provide them with a selection of filter materials to choose from and a number of suitable containers, such as large plant pots, garden sieves, a punctured bucket, or large foil food trays with holes punched in them, to provide structure for their filter beds. Display Resource sheet 2: Filter bed instructions and model the process of making one type of filter bed using <u>some</u> of the possible materials. This method will take the cleansing process so far, but further action will be needed to make the water as clean as possible. Encourage children to use their own ideas as they develop a process. If necessary, suggest using wadding and other materials to refine the process and clean the contaminated water more effectively in the latter stages.

Prompt their thinking by asking: How will you remove the largest particles from the water? What types of materials will you put into your filter beds? How will you remove the tiniest particles? How many times will you need to filter the water?

They should plan how they will filter the water and work together to achieve as clean water as possible. Tell them to make notes about the sequence of filtering, and the materials they used that are most effective, as these will form the basis of their recommendations.

Pupil Workbook: Complete Activity 2: Filtering water on pages 74 and 75.

Adaptations and support

Provide a bowl or bucket of contaminated water and a selection of sieves, filters and filter papers that children can use to clean their contaminated water sample. Ask children to discuss the sequence of their process and decide what to use. They should photograph each step in the cleaning sequence.

Give each group Resource sheet 1: Process planner to write notes about what they will do.

Take it further

Children should use microscopes to check for particles not visible to the naked eye. What does this tell them about how clean the water is?

Reflect and review

Tell each group to discuss, then sum up the main findings from their investigation in a poster, flow chart or labelled diagram.

Remind children of the lesson question, **'How can we clean up contaminated water?'** Ask one child from each group to share their method and describe what parts of the process seemed to work best. Ask: What were the most effective filters? Draw the children's thinking together with the aim of achieving a consensus practical method.

Was the water completely clean? Was it clear or was it still slightly cloudy? Could any remaining solids be dissolved in it? How could you test it to see if it has solids dissolved in it? Remind them of the observations of the evaporated solutions they observed at the beginning of the lesson.

Children who completed the **Take it further** task should share their learning at this point. Ask: What could you see through the microscope in the filtered water?

Ensure that they suggest stages and methods that will remove visible contamination from the water, and that they recognise that this 'clean water' will still not be safe to drink.

Pupil Workbook: Complete Activity 3: Reflect and review on page 76.

Answers

How can we clean up contaminated water?

By using a sequence of increasingly fine grade filters.

How could you test if the water still has solids dissolved in it?

Using a finer grade filter e.g. filter paper or evaporating the water.

Homework suggestions

Children could find out about different water filters. What are the water filters used in water systems, water jugs, in houses and swimming pools made from? What other treatments could be used?

Assessment and evidence of learning

Children can:

- identify different processes that might be useful in cleaning up contaminated water, using their prior knowledge of separating mixtures
- select appropriate resources to use to make a filter system
- test, review and improve methods, evaluating which are most effective
- explain the most effective methods to use to clean up contaminated water
- explain that clear water is not necessarily clean and must be treated to remove impurities.

Lesson 5: What makes a change non-reversible?

What children will learn and do

- Children learn that some changes of state are physical and reversible, while others are chemical and non-reversible.
- They test different combinations of materials that change chemically to produce carbon dioxide gas.
- They control variables to ensure they can trust their results.
- They record evidence to help them decide which is the best mixture of materials.
- They answer the lesson question: **'What makes a change non-reversible?'**

You will need

- disposable gloves, one per group (Biodegradable types of gloves are now readily available – these are compostable and degrade in around five years, compared to 50 years for other types. It is often possible to reuse the gloves after inflating, keeping them for further similar activities.)
- solids: bicarbonate of soda, tartaric acid, baking powder, effervescent vitamin C tablets, effervescent indigestion tablets
- liquids: water, white vinegar, lemon juice
- small beakers, cups, teaspoons
- reusable small plastic bottles, one per group

If using the Snap Science Year 5 Pupil Workbook you may not require the resource sheet below.

Snap Science Year 5 Pupil Workbook

- pages 77–78

Snap Science Year 5 Digital subscription

- Interactive 1: Busy kitchen image
- Resource sheet 1: Non-reversible mixtures checklist (optional)
- Interactive 2: Reversible or non-reversible? Physical or chemical?
- Snapshot 1: Reversible change

Make sure you have opened/printed any *Snap* resources you intend to use in this lesson.

National Curriculum

Conceptual knowledge:

- demonstrate that dissolving, mixing and changes of state are reversible changes
- explain that some changes result in the formation of new materials and that this kind of change is not usually reversible, including changes associated with [burning and] the action of acid on bicarbonate of soda

Working scientifically:

- planning different types of scientific enquiries to answer questions, including recognising, and controlling variables, where necessary

Scientific enquiry type:

- comparative testing

Key vocabulary	
Tier 2 vocabulary:	**Tier 3 vocabulary:**
Inflate	comparative test, conclusion, observe/observation, variable carbon dioxide, gas, liquid, non-reversible, reversible, solid

Health and safety Please refer to CLEAPSS for Health and Safety guidance and ensure that any identified hazards are managed appropriately.

Getting started

Tell children that today's lesson question is **'What makes a change non-reversible?'**

Remind children of the term reversible change. Check that they understand what it means and can give some examples of that type of change from earlier lessons. Introduce a new term, non-reversible (also called irreversible) change, to describe a change to a material or materials, where the original material/s cannot be brought back.

Show children Interactive 1: Busy kitchen image, featuring numerous materials in different stages of change.

Tell children to talk about the Busy kitchen image with their partner. Encourage them to identify examples of materials and whether they have changed (or are about to).

Ask: What is changing? How will it change? Do you think the original material/s could be brought back?

Encourage children to give reasons for their answers. Click on the interactive to reveal whether the changes identified are reversible or non-reversible.

Explain that during this lesson they are going to investigate a non-reversible change. Show them some bicarbonate of soda (a solid) and white vinegar (a liquid). Ask one child to smell each one and then ask again: What do you think they are? Establish that the bicarbonate of soda is not salt or sugar and that the vinegar is not water.

Add the vinegar to the bicarbonate of soda and ask children to observe very carefully what happens. Establish that bubbles are given off, and these contain a gas. Explain that a chemical change has taken place and a new material, carbon dioxide gas has been produced. The change that has taken place cannot be reversed – it is non-reversible.

Demonstrate how to inflate a disposable glove using the carbon dioxide gas produced by mixing bicarbonate of soda and white vinegar. Use a small plastic bottle , and elastic bands to fasten the glove to the bottle.

Place about 50 ml of white vinegar in the bottle and about two tablespoons of bicarbonate of soda in the glove. Take care to shake the powder into the fingers of the glove. Attach the glove to the rim of the bottle with an elastic band, without tipping any powder into the bottle at this stage. Tell children to observe carefully what happens as the solid combines with the liquid. When everyone is ready, shake the powder from the glove fingers into the bottle. Time how long it takes for the glove to stand upright and wave to the class.

Ask: What made the glove expand? Where did the gas come from? What type of change was this? Why?

Tell children that they are going to carry out a comparative test to find out which is the best mixture for producing gas to inflate a glove.

Pupil Workbook: Complete Activity 1: Reversible and non-reversible changes on page 77.

The task

Provide children, working in small groups, with beakers and a selection of solids and liquids to use as they carry out some initial tests to find out which mixture produces the most gas. Remind them, as they work as scientists, to be systematic, changing only one variable at a time, for example, using the same volume of vinegar each time while changing the solid used, or changing the liquid used while keeping the type and amount of solid the same. They should devise a way to record the different mixtures they test and their observations of the amount of gas produced.

Once they have identified the mixture that produced the most gas the children should then test out their chosen mixture, using a glove, and adjusting the proportions of solid and liquid as necessary. They should add a conclusion to summarise the results of this final test to their record.

Pupil Workbook: Complete Activity 2: Which mixture produces the most gas? on pages 77 and 78.

Adaptations and support

Provide children with a limited selection of materials and Resource sheet 1: Non-reversible mixtures checklist to help them structure their test.

Take it further

Tell children that you have a recipe which suggests that 30 g of bicarbonate of soda and 50 ml of white vinegar should be enough to inflate a disposable glove. If this is the case (and they will need to check), how much of each material will they need to inflate other things? Provide children with a variety of balloons of different sizes and shapes, plus some plastic bags of different sizes, to test.

Reflect and review

Ask children to share which mixture they found to be most effective at inflating their disposable glove. Encourage them to refer to their results for evidence, explaining which materials were most successful and how they know.

Revisit the lesson question: **'What makes a change non-reversible?'** Ensure that children recognise that a chemical change has taken place and that a new material has been produced. The original materials cannot be restored.

Tell children that you need to inflate some balloons. What would be the best way for you to do it? Display Interactive 2: Reversible or non-reversible? Physical or chemical?.

Explain that there are a number of options on screen, such as using a foot pump or a mix of chemicals or heating the air up, and that together you are going to sort them into reversible or non-reversible changes.

Ask*:* Can you think of any other examples of non-reversible changes? To prompt their thinking, refer back to the Busy kitchen image (used earlier in the lesson), which includes several other examples of changes, such as baking and toasting bread (colour and texture change) and frying an egg (uncooked to cooked, liquid to solid change). They might also suggest burning materials in a bonfire or lighting a candle.

Answers

What is a reversible change?

A reversible change is a physical change. For example, they might say, 'Some materials change physically when they are heated or cooled, or when they are mixed with other materials. Nothing has changed permanently, and nothing has been made, like a gas. The materials can be separated out using different methods like sieving, filtering and evaporating'.

What is a non-reversible change?

A non-reversible change is a chemical change where a new material is made. For example, they might say 'When some materials are combined, they change and produce new materials, such as carbon dioxide gas.'

Homework suggestions

Tell children to make a list of reversible and non-reversible changes they can identify around their homes. On return to school ask them to share their observations, making sure that the examples they give of non-reversible changes are accurate.

Assessment and evidence of learning

Children can:

- observe how materials change when mixed together and a chemical, non-reversible change takes place
- identify the most effective mix of and proportion between materials, to produce the most carbon dioxide gas, and inflate a disposable glove
- explain what happens to a mixture of materials when a physical, reversible change takes place. They can give examples and describe ways in which a physical, reversible change can be reversed using simple methods such as sieving, filtering or evaporating
- explain what happens to a mixture of materials when a chemical, non-reversible change takes place. They can give examples of non-reversible changes and state that these types of change cannot be reversed, because new materials have been made.

If you are unsure whether a child knows the differences between reversible and non-reversible changes you can use Snapshot 1: Reversible change to check understanding and develop their learning.

Lesson 6: How much gas can be produced by a non-reversible change?

What children will learn and do

- Children learn that non-reversible changes result in the formation of new materials, in this case carbon dioxide gas.
- They test different combinations of materials to make 'rocket fuel'.
- They present their findings in a newspaper headline.
- They answer the lesson question: **'How much gas can be produced by a non-reversible change?'**

You will need

- narrow measuring cylinders or small beakers
- water in jugs
- effervescent vitamin C tablets (one per group)
- small containers with snap-on lids e.g. small film canisters or other plastic storage pots (one per group). Film canisters are difficult to source for free now, but can be bought in bulk on line quite cheaply, washed and used multiple times
- plastic trays (one per group)
- weighing scales
- tape measures
- sticky tack
- reference materials for research (**Take it further** task)

If using the Snap Science Year 5 Pupil Workbook you may not require the resource sheet below.

Snap Science Year 5 Pupil Workbook

- pages 79–80

Snap Science Year 5 Digital subscription

- Resource sheet 1: Concept sentences
- Lesson 5 Snapshot1: Reversible change

Make sure you have opened/printed any *Snap* resources you intend to use in this lesson.

National Curriculum

Conceptual knowledge:

- explain that some changes result in the formation of new materials and that this kind of change is not usually reversible, including changes associated with burning and the action of acid on bicarbonate of soda

Working scientifically:

- planning different types of scientific enquiries to answer questions, including recognising, and controlling variables, where necessary
- using test results to make predictions to set up further [comparative and] fair tests

Scientific enquiry type:

- fair testing

Key vocabulary	
Tier 2 vocabulary:	**Tier 3 vocabulary:** fair test, conclusion, predict/prediction, variable carbon dioxide, non-reversible, reversible

Health and safety Please refer to CLEAPSS for Health and Safety guidance and ensure that any identified hazards are managed appropriately.

Getting started

Ask children to look back at their conclusions from the last lesson. Ask: What type of change took place when you inflated the disposable glove? Why was that change non-reversible?

Give each group of three children one Vitamin C tablet and a beaker or measuring cylinder containing a small amount of water. Tell them to use what they know already to predict what might happen when they break off and add a small piece of tablet to the water. They should check their ideas by observing what happens as they build up gradually to add a full tablet.

Ask: What do you notice happening?

Give children a set of Resource sheet 1: Concept sentences per group and ask them to use the words to create a sentence describing the process that has taken place.

Tell children that in this lesson they will be using their knowledge of gas-producing mixtures to help them launch a pocket-sized 'rocket' and answer the lesson question: **'How much gas can be produced by a non-reversible change?'**

First, show children how to use a small container with a lid to make a simple rocket that they will be able to adapt later. The container and lid need to be as dry as possible and a snug fit. Put a small amount of water in the bottom of the container and stick a blob of sticky tack inside the lid. Push the tablet into the sticky tack, to keep it away from the water until you are ready to set off the rocket. Quickly turn the container upside down and place it on its lid in a plastic tray. Stand well back. Talk about what they noticed and what they think caused the container to fly up.

Ask: How will changing the amount of water or Vitamin C tablet affect how high the pocket-sized rocket flies?

Pupil Workbook: Complete Activity 1: Non-reversible changes on page 79.

The task

Children work in small groups to choose a variable to test and plan a fair test, predicting when the rocket will fly highest. They will need to agree how to measure how high the canister flies, perhaps appointing someone to mark on a wall the point at which the rocket starts to fall.

Ask children to remind you of the success criteria for a fair test: to change only one thing at a time -- the independent variable; keep everything else the same -- control variables; measure or observe the outcome – dependent variable.

Children carry out their fair test, recording their results in a table. Warn children not to return to their rocket before it has taken off. They evaluate the prediction they made and identify any further testing that might be necessary.

Pupil Workbook: Complete Activity 2: Planning a fair test on page 79 and Activity 3: Results and conclusion on page 80.

Adaptations and support

Support children where necessary as they identify variables to change, measure and control; decide how to collect and present data; interpret and communicate their findings.

Take it further

Ask children to use secondary sources of information to find out more about rockets in real life, such as those used for research, space travel and exploration. Encourage them to focus on how these rockets move, how far they can travel, and what fuels they use. Tell them to summarise what they learn about the work of scientists in developing these rockets in a poster or annotated diagram.

Reflect and review

Ask each group to complete the following newspaper headline:

Breaking news: Best Ever Rocket Fuel Invented – just mix together ...

Revisit the lesson question: **'How much gas can be produced by a non-reversible change?'** Ask: Which mixture produced the most gas? How do you know? Encourage children to refer to their data and detail the most effective mixture of tablet to water used in powering their pocket-sized rockets.

Remind them that they tested a very narrow range of materials (water and effervescent Vitamin C tablets) in today's test and ask them whether they think that there might be a better mix, referring them back to data they collected during the last lesson. Prompt them by suggesting other mixes of liquid and solid, such as bicarbonate of soda and vinegar. Ask children to make a prediction based on the combined data from Lessons 5 and 6 and to frame a further scientific question to investigate their ideas more fully, for example, 'We predict that a mixture of bicarbonate of soda and vinegar will make the rocket fly higher. Our question to investigate will be: How high will a mixture of bicarbonate of soda and vinegar make our rocket fly?'

Answers

Using the concept sentence cards

Example: 'The solid tablet and liquid water change when mixed and rapidly produce gas'

Variables

- amount and type of liquid
- amount of Vitamin C tablet

Why does the canister launch into the air?

The water and Vitamin C tablet mix and a chemical, non-reversible change takes place. A gas is produced. The gas takes up more space that the liquid and tablet did so it pushes on the container's wall and lid. The weakest spot is the seal where the lid fits on and the gas forces it open, pushing the container into the air.

How much gas can be produced by a non-reversible change?

Children test a specific combination of materials in this lesson, investigating the proportion of effervescent tablet to water. The capacity of snap-on lidded containers tends to be small and that will be a limiting factor in this case. There is an optimum amount of tablet that will produce the greatest pressure in the container and lift to the rocket as a consequence.

Homework suggestions

With an adult at home, look online for a video of 'the Coke and Mentos' experiment. Explain to the adult what type of change is happening.

Assessment and evidence of learning

Children can:

- recognise variables that might be changed, need to stay the same, should be observed or measured in order to answer their question
- record data in sufficient detail to identify the amount of different materials that produces the most gas
- explain that the changes they have observed are non-reversible and that carbon dioxide has been produced as a result of the chemical reaction that has taken place

If you are unsure whether a child knows the differences between reversible and non-reversible changes you can use Lesson 5 Snapshot 1: Reversible change to check understanding and develop their learning.

Module 6: Human growth and reproduction

Lesson 1: How do newborn babies change into teenagers?

What children will learn and do

- Children learn about the different developmental stages in humans from newborn to teenager – physical changes and capabilities, social and learning.
- They interview experts to gather information.
- They sequence the developmental stages of children as a 'milestones chart'.
- They answer the lesson question: **'How do newborn babies change into teenagers?'**

You will need

- camera (optional)
- set of photographs of children at different ages (optional)

If using the Snap Science Year 5 Pupil Workbook you may not require the resource sheet below.

Snap Science Year 5 Pupil Workbook

- pages 81–83

Snap Science Year 5 Digital subscription

- Slideshow 1: Where does the baby grow?
- Resource sheet 1: Human development milestones

Make sure you have opened/printed any *Snap* resources you intend to use in this lesson.

Resource sheet 1: Human development milestones should be printed on A3 paper.

Before the lesson, arrange a visit from a mother and baby below the age of 2. Interview the mother about what the baby can do for themself and what they need help with and ask the children to take notes. Find out how the baby has changed since they were born. Label these notes 'Infancy: Ages 0-2 years'.

As part of this lesson, arrange to interview a teacher or TA from Early Years.

National Curriculum

Conceptual knowledge:

- describe the changes in humans to old age

Working scientifically:

- reporting and presenting findings from enquiries, including conclusions, causal relationships and explanations of [and degree of trust in results, in oral and] written forms such as displays and other presentations

Scientific enquiry type:

- finding things out using a wide range of secondary sources

Key vocabulary	
Tier 2 vocabulary:	**Tier 3 vocabulary:**
milestone, stage, system	abdomen, childhood, gestation, infancy, large intestine, life cycle, mammal, newborn, oesophagus, organs, pregnancy, reproduction, small intestine, stomach, teenager, umbilical cord, uterus

Health and safety Please refer to CLEAPSS for Health and Safety guidance and ensure that any identified hazards are managed appropriately.

Getting started

Introduce the topic by asking children how they have changed since they were a baby. Ask: What can you do now that you couldn't do when you were born? Or when you started school?

Tell children that these changes are part of the human life cycle and that they happen in distinct stages, starting when a human is still growing inside their mother. Remind children that humans are mammals. What have they learnt about how mammals are different from other types of animals eg. birds, or fish? Remind them that mammals give birth to live young.

Ask: Have you ever seen a pet or farm animal give birth? Display Slideshow 1: Where does the baby grow?

Show the first slide on the slide show of a ewe giving birth. Discuss what they have seen. Avoid lingering on the pain of childbirth and instead focus on the mother's body pushing the baby out of a hole at the rear end of the animal.

Tell children that in order to understand where the baby has grown inside the body we will need to understand more about the part of the body involved. This stage of the human life cycle is called gestation. When a woman is growing a baby inside her body she is pregnant and this stage is called pregnancy.

Talk through the slides one by one.

Slide 2: The baby grows in the lower part of the female body – the abdomen.

Slide 3: There are many organs inside the female body – lungs, heart, digestive system etc. Ask children to locate the parts of the digestive system.

Slide 4: Point to the parts of the digestive system they learnt about in Year 4 (mouth, oesophagus, stomach, small and large intestines). The reproductive system is different. Locate the uterus and explain that this is where the baby grows. The uterus has to stretch as the baby grows but it returns to its original size after the baby is born.

Slide 5: The baby is attached to the mother by the umbilical cord so it doesn't need to breathe or eat for itself. The food eaten by the mother and the oxygen breathed in by the mother reach the baby in blood which passes through the umbilical cord.

Slide 6: When the baby is born, it can breathe and feed as we do. The umbilical cord is cut at birth as it is not needed any longer. The scar from this is our 'belly button'.

The next stage is infancy. This starts at the moment of birth and continues to the age of about two. It includes babies and toddlers.

Recap on the visit from a mother and baby (arranged to happen before this lesson). Remind them how old the baby was. Ask: What is the baby able to do for itself? What does the baby learn to do in this stage? How long could a child at this stage of its lifecycle be independent/left alone for?

Pupil Workbook: Complete Activity 1: How have I changed? on page 81, Activity 2: Gestation on page 81, Activity 3: Infancy on page 81 and Activity 4: Childhood on page 81.

The task

Tell children that in this lesson they are going to answer today's lesson question: **'How do newborn babies change into teenagers?'**

Tell children: Your task in this lesson is to create a chart of all the developments made by a child as they grow from a newborn to a teenager. They will use the notes they took during the visit from a mother and baby and plus interview an expert.

Give each child a copy of Resource sheet 1: Human development milestones on a piece of A3 paper. Look at the information box on the sheet. Ask: Can you find something in your notes from the baby visit which fits into these categories?

Body Changes: (leg length, height and change in teeth, hair)

Physical Abilities: (sitting, crawling, walking, running, talking, riding a bike)

Self-Care: (feeding, dressing, bathing, brushing teeth, walking to a shop with no adult)

Learning:(reading, writing, painting, learning about the world, learning about history)

Tell children that they will begin by putting their notes from the baby visit onto this chart. Show children how to summarise a change into a statement e.g. Babies cut their first teeth. Tell children to write this into the 'Infancy: Ages 0-2' of the milestone chart. Give them time to fill the first five boxes on the chart with their information collected from the baby visit.

Tell children that they will be taking more notes in this lesson, to put on their charts. To gather this information, we will be interviewing adults who work with children aged 3-5, the stage called early childhood.

Invite your visitors into the room or link up via a video call. Ask the following questions to start the process and then allow children to ask follow-up questions to find out more about the children's development at nursery school age and reception class:

Questions to ask the EYFS teacher/TA:

- How old are the children in your class?
- Can they write their name?
- Can they read a book?
- Can they clean their own teeth?
- Can they go to the toilet on their own?
- Can they ride a bike with 2 wheels?
- Can they go to the shops on their own?
- Can they make their own dinner?
- Can they use a knife and fork to cut up their own dinner?

Make sure that the answers given show a progression in these skills. Tell children to use their notes to add information to the boxes labelled 'Early Childhood: Age 3-5 years'.

Tell children to add a new section to their notes: 'Later Childhood: Ages 6–12 years'. Ask children:

- What has changed about you since you were 5?
- What can you do now that you couldn't do when you were 5?
- What do you do to take responsibility for yourself or care for yourself that you couldn't do at 5?
- What sort of things do you learn about in school now that you couldn't have understood when you were 5?

Use these questions to generate some ideas for discussion. Tell children to write notes during the discussion then transfer their chosen ideas to the chart in the last section: 'Later Childhood: Ages 6-12 years'.

Pupil Workbook: Complete Activity 5: Human development milestones on page 83.

Adaptations and support

The chart could be replaced with a set of photographs of children at different ages that they sequence and annotate.

Take it further

Some children could also take a height measurement from all the age groups you interview and plot this on a line graph. Remind children that there are 12 months in every year so they should have a scale that works with 12s.

Reflect and review

Display all the charts around the classroom. Ask children to view each other's work. Once they have seen a variety of charts, ask them if there is anything they wish they had added to their own chart and then give them time to neatly add this information.

Ask: Did you find out anything that you didn't know before?

Ask them if they found an answer to today's lesson question: **'How do newborn babies change into teenagers?'** What scientific ways of working have they used to answer the question?

Answers

The exact information does not matter as much as showing that the child changes over time.

For ages 0-2 it could include:

- sits up
- crawls
- walks
- copies sounds
- claps hands
- says words
- holds own drink

For ages 3-5 it could include:

- points
- talks in sentences
- plays make-believe games
- climbs
- follows simple instructions
- tells stories
- draws pictures

For ages 4-6 it might include learning to:

- ride a bike
- read
- brush own teeth
- make own breakfast
- recite 2 x table
- get dressed
- swim

For ages 6-12 it might include learning to:

- go to the shops alone
- put self to bed
- read a novel
- wash own hair/take shower
- learn about history/geography/science
- make a snack
- learn a part in a play
- swim in the deep end

They used secondary sources of information to find out about child development (asking experts – mother and teacher/TA) and made their own observations.

Homework suggestions

Children could find out when other baby mammals develop? Find out when a lamb first walks? When does a kitten stop drinking its mother's milk? When does a fox kitten stop living with its mother?

Assessment and evidence of learning

Children can:

- state that a baby develops in the uterus of a woman, not the stomach
- describe some of the developmental changes from newborn to teenagers
- sequence the developmental stages of children that they have observed as a 'milestones chart'.

Lesson 2: How do girls become women?

This is the first part of a two-part lesson. In this lesson children learn about the life cycle stage of puberty in girls. By the end of this lesson they will know about some of the physical changes involved. In Lesson 3 children learn about puberty in boys. These lessons can be taught to mixed or single gender groups but all children should learn about changes in boys and girls.

This lesson covers only the science aspects of a Sex and Relationships Education (SRE) programme; some questions and issues arising from it may be more appropriately addressed in PSHE lessons. Reference should be made to the school's SRE policy.

What children will learn and do

- Children learn that the female body changes as it goes through puberty – from about age 12.
- They learn that there is a fast period of growth and that changes occur that prepare women to have babies.
- They make a poster to inform young people about these changes.
- They answer the lesson question: **'How do girls become women?'**

You will need

- pens and pencils (enough for all children)
- pre-prepared question box to collect questions – needs to be postbox style to ensure questions are secure inside
- age-appropriate books, websites or other resources on puberty

If using the Snap Science Year 5 Pupil Workbook you may not require all the resource sheets below.

Snap Science Year 5 Pupil Workbook

- pages 84–85

Snap Science Year 5 Digital subscription

- Slideshow 1: Arms in the air!
- Resource sheet 1: Woman or girl?
- Animation 1: The changes that happen to a girl during puberty
- Resource sheet 2: Girl to woman (A3 size)

Make sure you have opened/printed any *Snap* resources you intend to use in this lesson.

National Curriculum

Conceptual knowledge:

- describe the changes in humans to old age

Working scientifically:

- reporting and presenting findings from enquiries, including conclusions, causal relationships and explanations of [and degree of trust in results], in oral and [written forms such as displays and other presentations

Key vocabulary	
Tier 2 vocabulary:	**Tier 3 vocabulary:** breasts, genitals, hygiene, life cycle, menstruation/having a period, puberty, pubic hair, sweat, vagina

Health and safety Please refer to CLEAPSS for Health and Safety guidance and ensure that any identified hazards are managed appropriately.

Getting started

Look at one of the milestone charts made in the previous lesson. Recap on the ways that newborn babies change in order to become teenagers. One of the most obvious changes is the length of our arms and legs compared to the rest of our bodies. Display Slideshow 1: Arms in the air! and note the different limb lengths. Ask: What else about these children has changed?

Explain that the next two lessons will be looking at the changes from teenager to adult, and that this stage of the human life cycle is called puberty. Remind children about the ground rules that are used in PSHE lessons, including the use of correct vocabulary where known, rather than family or playground words.

Display Resource sheet 1: Woman or girl? and ask children to decide which images show girls and which show women. Discuss what characteristics the girls/women have. Remind children that some of them may not be visible in the pictures. Take feedback from the class, list the features that have been identified and challenge any misconceptions. Children may already be familiar with some changes if your SRE programme introduces them in earlier year groups.

Tell children that, in this lesson, they will be finding the answer to the lesson question: **'How do girls become women?'**

Pupil Workbook: Complete Activity 1: Girls and women on page 84.

The task

Show and discuss Animation 1: The changes that happen to a girl during puberty. Ensure that children know that although the cartoon shows a white girl, all girls go through puberty. Follow school policy for dealing with questions about content not included in the Key Stage 2 science programme of study; you may need to tell children that they will learn this when they are older or that it will be covered in PSHE. You could note any questions and put them in a question box to be discussed in the appropriate lesson.

Tell children that they will be presenting information and advice about puberty in girls on a poster.

Give each child an A3 copy of Resource sheet 2: Girl to woman. Spend a few minutes discussing what they know about the changes from girl to woman. Ask: What is the reason girls need to change in this way when they become women? Which of these changes usually happen first/last? Are you using the correct scientific words and explaining what they mean?

Tell the children that their task is to produce a poster with the title 'Things all girls need to know by the age of 10', for display in a school.

They should annotate it to show the main physical changes, including information about the significance of the changes, such as breasts produce milk for babies, and any useful advice, such as about personal hygiene. Remind them that they do not need to add any drawings, just information in the boxes and labelling lines.

They can also use the books and other resources you have provided to find information and check facts.

The animation they saw earlier offers tampons and pads as the two ways to deal with period blood. However, there are other options to choose from nowadays and many are washable and thus reusable. Absorbent period pants are one of the easiest ways to deal with periods and could be offered here as an alternative which is much better for the environment and easier to wear. You may want to discuss this before making the posters.

Once the posters have been completed, check for misconceptions and inappropriate wording first and then display the posters on desks, allowing the children to see each other's work and consider their factualness, clarity and design. Allow time to give feedback to one another about what was good about their work.

Pupil Workbook: Complete Activity 2: Girl to woman on page 85.

Adaptations and support

The annotations for the poster could be annotated orally by recording a voiceover for a video of the image of the picture.

Take it further

Consider for a moment, what it would be like to have no access to sanitary products. Girls living in extreme poverty may not have access and this can affect their education if they are unable to go to school when they have their period. This is known as period poverty.

Tell children that in many workplaces, sanitary products are made available for anyone to use. Having them freely available at work helps to improve equality between the sexes.

In the same way, women are given paid maternity leave when they take time off work to have a baby or adopt a child. Increasingly, a couple of weeks of paid leave is given to partners too. Ask them to consider what else might be different about the experiences of men and women as a result of their reproductive functions. Ask: How could we make these experiences fair for all?

Reflect and review

Ask children if they have found the answer to the lesson question: **'How do girls become women?'**

Tell children that humans go through many times of change in their lives. They have already changed a lot since they were born. All of those changes are completely normal and soon the changes of puberty will feel normal too.

Ask for two or three children to volunteer to sit in the 'hot seat' as experts on female puberty. The others ask questions about changes that occur to girls at this stage of the life cycle. Encourage children to add further information to the answers the experts provide. If no children volunteer you can take the 'hot seat'.

Remind children that now, or later when they have had time to think about it, they can add further questions to the question box. You will need to find a time (probably in a related PSHE lesson or circle time) to answer them.

Tell children that they should not disclose publicly sensitive information about themselves or others. If they are worried by anything in the lesson or by anything they are asked to do by an adult or older child they should discuss it privately with an appropriate adult. Children who do share information must be told that you cannot guarantee to keep it confidential: if a child discloses something of concern it must be reported to the member of staff responsible for child protection.

Answers

Changes from girl to woman:

- Growth spurt
- Pubic hair grows in groin
- Hair grows under arms
- Breasts develop
- Hips widen
- Voice lowers
- Sweat production increases (Body odour)
- Sebum production increases (spots)
- Period/ menstruation begins

Homework suggestions

No suggested homework is assigned for this lesson.

Assessment and evidence of learning

Children can:

- identify the main visible differences between a girl and a woman
- identify the main changes of the stage of the human life cycle that occur at puberty in girls
- give reasons for some of the changes that occur
- present what they have learnt from the animation and discussion in the poster.

Lesson 3: How do boys become men?

This is the second part of a two-part lesson. In this lesson children learn about the life cycle stage of puberty in boys. By the end of this lesson they will know about some of the physical changes involved. In Lesson 2 children learnt about puberty in girls. These lessons can be taught to mixed or single gender groups but all children should learn about changes in boys and girls.

This lesson covers only the science aspects of a Sex and Relationships Education (SRE) programme; some questions and issues arising from it may be more appropriately addressed in PSHE lessons. Reference should be made to the school's SRE policy.

What children will learn and do

- Children learn that the male body changes as it goes through puberty – from about age 12.
- They make a poster to inform young people about these changes.
- They answer the lesson question: **'How do boys become men?'**

You will need

- pre-cut cards or scissors (one per child)
- glue sticks (one per pair)
- age-appropriate books, websites, or other resources on puberty

If using the Snap Science Year 5 Pupil Workbook you may not require all the resource sheets below.

Snap Science Year 5 Pupil Workbook

- pages 86–87

Snap Science Year 5 Digital subscription

- Lesson 2 Slideshow 1: Arms in the air!
- Resource sheet 1: Man or boy?
- Animation 1: The changes that happen to a boy during puberty
- Resource sheet 2: Changes cards (1 set per pair)
- Resource sheet 3: Male puberty (A3 size)
- Resource sheet 4: Email from an alien (optional)

Make sure you have opened/printed any *Snap* resources you intend to use in this lesson.

National Curriculum

Conceptual knowledge:

- describe the changes in humans to old age

Working scientifically:

- reporting and presenting findings from enquiries, including conclusions, causal relationships and explanations of [and degree of trust in results, in oral and] written forms such as displays and other presentations.

Key vocabulary	
Tier 2 vocabulary:	Tier 3 vocabulary: Adam's apple, genitals, life cycle, muscles, puberty, pubic hair

Health and safety Please refer to CLEAPSS for Health and Safety guidance and ensure that any identified hazards are managed appropriately.

Getting started

Remind children that in the previous lesson, they learned about the stage in the human life cycle when girls change to become women. Remind them that this stage is called puberty and that while it generally starts about age 12, each person's development is unique and that the onset and duration of puberty can vary significantly among individuals.

Display Lesson 2 Slideshow 1: Arms in the air! Recap on the fact that arm length changes a lot. Tell children that their legs also grow a great deal during the teenage years. It is this which accounts for most of their change in height during puberty. This growth can happen quite quickly so it is often called a growth spurt. For some people, this happens whilst they are still at primary school whilst others won't grow taller until they are 15 or 16.

Tell the children that this lesson is about boys. Remind children about the ground rules that are used in PSHE lessons, including the use of correct vocabulary where known, rather than family or playground words.

Display Resource sheet 1: Man or boy? and ask children to decide which images show boys and which show men. Discuss what characteristics the boys/men have. Remind children that some of them may not be visible in the pictures. Take feedback from the class, list the features that have been identified and challenge any misconceptions. Children may already be familiar with some changes if your SRE programme introduces them in earlier year groups.

Tell children that, in this lesson, they will be finding the answer to today's lesson question: **'How do boys become men?'**

Pupil Workbook: Complete Activity 1: Boys and men on page 86.

The task

Show and discuss Animation 1: The changes that happen to a boy during puberty. Ensure that children know that although the cartoon shows a white boy, all boys go through puberty. Follow school policy for dealing with questions about content not included in the Key Stage 2 science programme of study; you may need to tell children that they will learn this when they are older or that it will be covered in PSHE. You could note any questions and put them in a question box to be discussed in the appropriate lesson.

Give each pair of children Resource sheet 2: Changes cards pre-cut and ready to sort. Tell children that they are going to use these cards in three different sorting activities so nothing should be stuck down just yet.

1st Sorting Activity Instructions:

Remove the cards referring to girls only. (This could be an opportunity to address misconceptions.) Using only those which are relevant to boys, sort the cards into three piles: always true; sometimes true; I don't know.

Discuss the groups they have made.

2nd Sorting Activity Instructions:

Remove the cards referring to boys only. Using only those which are relevant to girls, sort the cards into three piles: always true; sometimes true; I don't know.

Discuss the groups they have made.

3rd Sorting Activity Instructions:

Sort the cards into three piles: only girls; only boys; both.

Discuss the groups they have made.

Make sure that children understand there are similarities and differences between puberty in individual boys and individual girls as well as between boys and girls.

Tell children to use these cards to annotate a drawing to show the changes that happen to boys during puberty. Give each pair Resource sheet 3: Male puberty and tell them they should use any relevant cards to label the diagram. They can now stick down the cards and join them to the relevant parts of the body with label lines. They can add any extra information which they feel is important.

They can also use the books and other resources you have provided to find information and check facts.

Ask: Does everyone change in the same way and at the same time? Where on the body does this change occur? Can you remember anything else about this? Have you described all the changes? Have you explained all the scientific words you have used?

Keep at least one of these posters to hand for Lesson 4 – What is the human life cycle?

Pupil Workbook: Complete Activity 2: Boy to man on page 87.

Adaptations and support

If the cards are pre-cut then they can be placed in position and glued. No additional text is required, especially if all children have been involved in the discussions.

Take it further

Provide children with Resource sheet 4: Email from an alien. They work individually or in pairs to write a description of puberty for the alien.

Reflect and review

Tell children that humans go through many times of change in their lives. They have already changed a lot since they were born. All those changes are completely normal and soon the changes of puberty will feel normal too.

Ask children if they have found the answer to today's lesson question: **'How do boys become men?'**

Ask children to consider what they have learned about puberty in boys and girls and to discuss with a partner which changes are specific to boys or girls and which happen to both. Summarise the discussions on a Venn diagram. Remind children that there are similarities and differences between puberty in individual boys and individual girls as well as between boys and girls.

Remind children that now, or later when they have had time to think about it, they can add further questions to the question box. You will need to find a time (probably in a related PSHE lesson or circle time) to answer them.

Tell children that they should not disclose publicly sensitive information about themselves or others. If they are worried by anything in the lesson or by anything they are asked to do by an adult or older child they should discuss it privately with an appropriate adult. Children who do share information must be told that you cannot guarantee to keep it confidential; if a child discloses something of concern it must be reported to the member of staff responsible for child protection.

Answers

1st sort: only those which are relevant to boys:

always true	sometimes	I don't know
The genitals grow bigger. Facial hair grows. Pubic hair grows around the genitals. Underarm hair grows in the armpits. The voice gradually gets deeper.	The body becomes very tall and broad. The muscles get bigger. The voice becomes squeaky. The chest becomes very hairy. The Adam's apple sticks out a long way. The back becomes hairy. The voice breaks. There is an increase in body hair. Spots form on the face. Puberty starts at about age 12. There are growth spurts.	

2nd sort: only those which are relevant to girls		
always true The voice gradually gets deeper. Pubic hair grows around the genitals. Underarm hair grows in the armpits.	**sometimes** There is an increase in body hair. There are growth spurts. Spots form on the face. Puberty starts at about age 12	**I don't know**
3rd sort:		
only girls	**only boys** The muscles get bigger. The genitals grow bigger The voice becomes squeaky. The chest becomes very hairy. Facial hair grows. The Adam's apple sticks out a long way. The back becomes hairy. The body becomes very tall and broad. Facial hair grows before the voice breaks.	**both** Pubic hair grows around the genitals. The voice gradually gets deeper. Underarm hair grows in the armpits. There is an increase in body hair. Spots form on the face. Puberty starts at about age 12. There are growth spurts.
A3 posters have all the cards appropriately placed next to the body part involved.		

Homework suggestions

Give children a common myth or misconception about puberty in either males and females or both (see module summary) and ask them to debunk it, explaining why the myth is false and providing evidence to support their argument.

Assessment and evidence of learning

Children can:

- identify the main visible differences between a boy and a man
- identify the main changes of the stage of the human life cycle that occur at puberty in boys
- present what they have learnt from the animation, wider reading and discussion in a poster.

Lesson 4: What is the human life cycle?

What children will learn and do

- Children learn that adulthood is the stage after puberty until old age. Adult bodies don't grow or change much. They are the strongest they will be in their lives and can reproduce.
- They learn that ageing starts from about middle adulthood; hair turns grey, skin becomes wrinkled and bodies get weaker.
- They learn that death is when the body stops working, and humans cannot move, think, breathe, feel, or do any of the things they used to do when they were alive.
- They decide the best way to represent the human life cycle diagrammatically.
- They answer the lesson question: **'What is the human life cycle?'**

You will need

- access to the internet
- photograph of yourself as a child
- if you have them – photographs of your parents as young people, adults and in old age
- suitable video of a time lapse of someone ageing
- scissors (one pair each)
- glue (enough for the class)
- one example each of the posters made in Lessons 2 and 3

If using the Snap Science Year 5 Pupil Workbook you may not require all the resource sheets below.

Snap Science Year 5 Pupil Workbook

- pages 88–91

Snap Science Year 5 Digital subscription

- Resource sheet 1: Age order
- Resource sheet 2: Phases of human life (cut into cards, one set per pair of children)
- Slideshow 1: Human life diagram
- Resource sheet 3: Using evidence
- Snapshot 1: Birth to old age

Make sure you have opened/printed any *Snap* resources you intend to use in this lesson.

National Curriculum

Conceptual knowledge:

- describe the changes as humans develop to old age

Working scientifically:

- reporting and presenting findings from enquiries, [including conclusions, causal relationships and explanations of and degree of trust in results,] in oral and written forms such as displays and other presentations

Key vocabulary	
Tier 2 vocabulary:	**Tier 3 vocabulary:**
Ageing	diagram, evidence gestation, life cycle, puberty, pregnancy

Health and safety Please refer to CLEAPSS for Health and Safety guidance and ensure that any identified hazards are managed appropriately.

Getting started

Display one of the posters from Lessons 2 and 3 explaining puberty. Recap on the changes that happen to boys and girls at this stage of the human life cycle. Tell children that we have now studied all the changes that happen on the way to becoming an adult. In adulthood, growth in height stops but other changes occur.

Find and display a time lapse of someone ageing on the internet. Watch the face change from child to adult and then watch the face shape, skin texture and amount of facial fat change again into old age. Ask children what they noticed.

If you have baby photographs, it is good to show them your own face as a child and discuss the changes. Avoid asking children to bring in baby photographs, as this can be problematic for looked-after children. You may have photographs of your parents as young people, adults and in old age which you could share. Ask: What changes as we grow older? Is there anything that you can't see that changes (movement, coordination, etc)?

Display Resource sheet 1: Age order.

Ask children to put the pictures in order according to the age of the person by numbering them from 1 for the youngest, and so on. Tell children to look for clues in the faces and bodies. Encourage children to suggest an order and then debate any they disagree on, using the sentence structure:

I think ____ is older than ____ because I can see that ________________.

Tell children:

- Adulthood is the stage after puberty until old age. Adult bodies don't grow or change much. They are the strongest they will be in their lives and can reproduce. Ageing starts from about middle adulthood; hair turns grey, skin becomes wrinkled and bodies get weaker. Older people tend to retire from work, sleep more and may not be able to do so much exercise as joints may be sore as they wear out. However, exercise, having fun with friends and keeping an active mind active can help older people to live well for longer.
- Death is when the body stops working, and humans cannot move, think, breathe, feel, or do any of the things they used to do when they were alive. It is a natural part of the cycle and although it is hard to imagine as a child, many old people feel very satisfied by the life they have led when they reach the end of their lives.

Tell children that these two stages are part of the human life cycle, just like all the other stages they have studied in the previous lessons.

Tell children that in this lesson they are going to find an answer to today's lesson question: **'What is the human life cycle?'**

Pupil Workbook: Complete Activity 1: Order the ages on page 88.

The task

Give each pair of children Resource sheet 2: Phases of human life and ask them to cut them into cards and match the phases to the images provided. Discuss any unfamiliar words and provide a definition.

Now ask children to put the terms (and images) in order. Ask them to consider whether this should be in the form of a straight line or a life cycle circle as they learnt to draw for other animals in Module 4.

Display Slideshow 1: Human life diagram. Discuss the three possible options. Ask: Which is the best and why? What labels should you add?

Display the chosen format and decide where the word cards from Resource sheet 2 should be placed. You could draw it on a whiteboard and begin to add some words to start them off.

Tell children to draw this diagram into their books/on paper and label it using the words from Resource sheet 2: in the correct positions.

Tell each pair to share the images from Resource sheet 2 with their partner so that each child has four cards. Give each child a copy of Resource sheet 3: Using evidence.

Tell children to stick their images at the top of the columns. Then they should look closely at each image, ignoring any differences in clothing, hairstyle and gender. Look for evidence of the age of each person. Estimate the age of the person in each of their chosen images and complete the table to record the evidence suggesting that age. Challenge them to use the words on the cards.

Pupil Workbook: Complete Activity 2: The phases of human life on page 89, Activity 3: Adulthood and old age on page 89, Activity 4: The human life cycle on page 90 and Activity 5: Using evidence to determine age on page 91.

Adaptations and support

Use the images from Resource sheet 2: Phases of human life. Four photographs could be annotated with simple words to reduce the writing content, rather than filling in the table on Resource sheet 3.

Take it further

Take a photograph of the face of each child and print it out. Using images of older people as a guide, children sketch onto the photograph. Tell them to include wrinkles, age spots and jowls to see what they might look like when they are older.

Reflect and review

Ask children if they have found an answer to today's lesson question: **'What is the human life cycle?'**

Ask them what kind of scientific recording methods they used to answer the question. Highlight the fact that they used a diagram and made choices about the best diagram to show the process. Scientists often have to figure out how best to show the ideas they are working on to other people and diagrams can be really helpful.

Give eight children each a card with one of the stages of the human life cycle on from Resource sheet 2. Tell them to arrange themselves as a life cycle. Ask the other children to check they are in the right place, and to ask them questions about what happens at the stage they are representing.

Tell children there are measures we can take to help us age well: regular exercise keeps our muscles strong and healthy; exercise also keeps our heart healthy; eating a varied and balanced diet will ensure we have all the vitamins and minerals we need to stay healthy; avoiding smoking is good for our health and for our skin – smoking gives you wrinkles; sun cream prevents our skin from wrinkling and getting age spots.

Answers

Life cycle diagram completed:

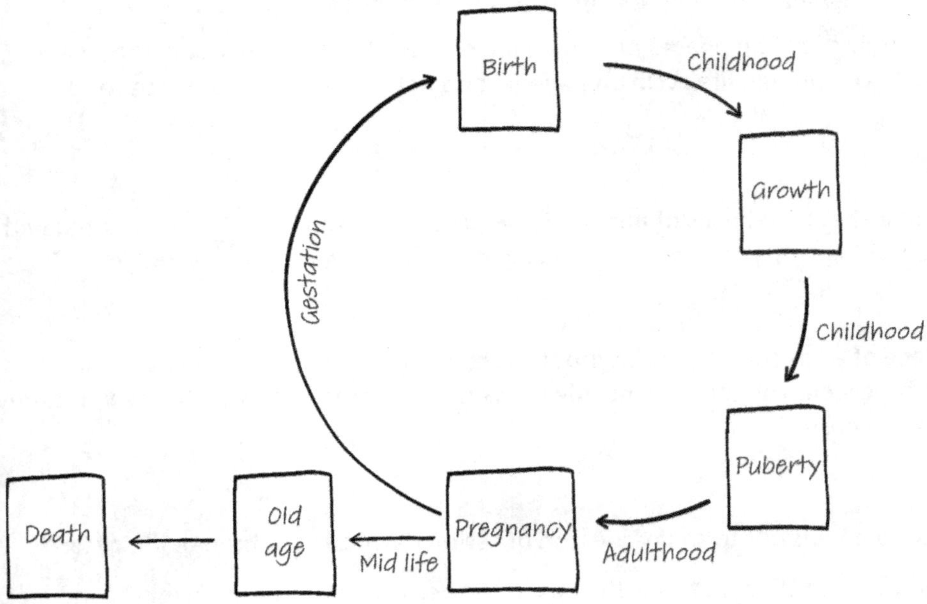

Example of an answer from Resource sheet 3:

I think this is a child aged less than 1.

Evidence:

milk teeth

crawling rather than walking

round face and clear skin

Homework suggestions

Children could write a letter to their future self, advising them on how to take care of themselves so they have a healthy old age.

Assessment and evidence of learning

Children can:

- describe the changes from birth to old age using the new words learnt, such as puberty and pregnancy
- order the phases of human life correctly
- draw an accurate life cycle for humans, making a sensible choice about which diagram best shows the life cycle.

If you are unsure if a child can describe the human life cycles, you can use Snapshot 1: Birth to old age.